THE DISCOMFORT ZONE

Jonathan Franzen won the National Book Award in 2001 for *The Corrections*, and is the author of two other critically acclaimed novels, *The Twenty-Seventh City* and *Strong Motion*, and a collection of essays, *How to Be Alone*. He lives in New York City and Boulder Creek, California.

THE
DISCOMFORT
ZONE

A PERSONAL HISTORY

JONATHAN FRANZEN

FOURTH ESTATE • London

This edition first published in Australia in 2006
First published in Great Britain in 2006
Fourth Estate
An imprint of HarperCollins*Publishers*
77–85 Fulham Palace Road
London W6 8JB
www.4thestate.co.uk

Jacket image: "Map of a Man's Heart" McCall's Magazine, January 1960, pp 32-33 Adapted from 19th Century originals by artist Jo Lowrey and the editors of McCall's

1 3 5 7 9 8 6 4 2

A catalogue record for this book is
available from the British Library

ISBN-13 978-0-00-724058-6
ISBN-10 0-00-724058-9

Set in Janson

Printed in Australia by Griffin Press, Australia

FOR

BOB AND **TOM**

CONTENTS

THE DISCOMFORT ZONE

HOUSE FOR SALE

THERE'D BEEN A STORM that evening in St. Louis. Water was standing in steaming black pools on the pavement outside the airport, and from the back seat of my taxi I could see oak limbs shifting against low-hanging urban clouds. The Saturday-night roads were saturated with a feeling of afterness, of lateness—the rain wasn't falling, it had already fallen.

My mother's house, in Webster Groves, was dark except for a lamp on a timer in the living room. Letting myself inside, I went directly to the liquor shelf and poured the hammer of a drink I'd been promising myself since before the first of my two flights. I had a Viking sense of entitlement to whatever provisions I could plunder. I was about to turn forty, and my older brothers had entrusted me with the job of traveling to Missouri and choosing a realtor to sell the house. For as long as I was in Webster Groves, doing work on behalf of the estate, the liquor shelf would be mine. Mine! Ditto the air-conditioning, which I set frostily low. Ditto the kitchen freezer, which I found it necessary to open immediately and get to the bottom of, hoping to discover some breakfast sausages, some homemade beef stew, some fatty and savory thing that I could warm up and eat before I went to bed. My mother had been good about labeling food with the date she'd frozen it. Beneath multiple bags of cranberries I found a package of small-mouth bass that a fisherman neighbor had caught three years earlier. Underneath the bass was a nine-year-old beef brisket.

I went through the house and stripped the family photos out of every room. I'd been looking forward to this work almost as much as to my drink. My mother had been too attached to the formality of her living room and dining room to clutter them with snapshots, but elsewhere each windowsill and each table-top was an eddy in which inexpensively framed photos had accumulated. I filled a shopping bag with the haul from the top of her TV cabinet. I picked another bag's worth from a wall of the family room, as from an espaliered fruit tree. Many of the pictures were of grandchildren, but I was represented in them, too—here flashing an orthodontic smile on a beach in Florida, here looking hungover at my college graduation, here hunching my shoulders on my ill-starred wedding day, here standing three feet away from the rest of my family during an Alaskan vacation that my mother, toward the end, had spent a substantial percentage of her life savings to take us on. The Alaskan picture was so flattering to nine of us that she'd applied a blue ballpoint pen to the eyes of the tenth, a daughter-in-law, who'd blinked for the photo and who now, with her misshapen ink-dot eyes, looked quietly monstrous or insane.

I told myself that I was doing important work by depersonalizing the house before the first realtor came to see it. But if somebody had asked me why it was also necessary, that same night, to pile the hundred-plus pictures on a table in the basement and to rip or slice or pry or slide each photo out of its frame, and then dump all the frames into shopping bags, and stow the shopping bags in cabinets, and shove all the photos into an envelope, so that nobody could see them—if somebody had pointed out my resemblance to a conqueror burning the enemy's churches and smashing its icons—I would have had to admit that I was relishing my ownership of the house.

I was the only person in the family who'd had a full childhood here. As a teenager, when my parents were going out, I'd counted the seconds until I could take temporary full possession of the house, and as long as they were gone I was sorry they were coming back. In the decades since, I'd observed the sclerotic buildup of family photographs resentfully, and I'd chafed at my mother's usurpation of my drawer and closet space, and when she'd asked me to clear out my old boxes of books and papers, I'd reacted like a house cat in whom she was trying to instill community spirit. She seemed to think she owned the place.

Which, of course, she did. This was the house where, five days a month for ten months, while my brothers and I were going about our coastal lives, she had come home alone from chemotherapy and crawled into bed. The house from which, a year after that, in early June, she had called me in New York and said she was returning to the hospital for more exploratory surgery, and then had broken down in tears and apologized for being such a disappointment to everyone and giving us more bad news. The house where, a week after her surgeon had shaken his head bitterly and sewn her abdomen back up, she'd grilled her most trusted daughter-in-law on the idea of an afterlife, and my sister-in-law had confessed that, in point of sheer logistics, the idea seemed to her pretty far-fetched, and my mother, agreeing with her, had then, as it were, put a check beside the item "Decide about afterlife" and continued down her to-do list in her usual pragmatic way, addressing other tasks that her decision had rendered more urgent than ever, such as "Invite best friends over one by one and say goodbye to them forever." This was the house from which, on a Saturday morning in July, my brother Bob had driven her to her hairdresser, who was Vietnamese and affordable and who greeted her with the words "Oh, Mrs. Fran, Mrs. Fran, you look *terrible*," and to which she'd returned, an hour later, to complete her makeover, because she was spending long-hoarded frequent-flyer miles on two first-class tickets, and first-class travel was an occasion for looking her best, which also translated into feeling her best; she came down from her bedroom dressed for first class, said good-bye to her sister, who had traveled from New York to ensure that the house would not be empty when my mother walked away from it—that someone would be left behind—and then went to the airport with my brother and flew to the Pacific Northwest for the rest of her life. Her house, being a house, was enough slower in its dying to be a zone of comfort to my mother, who needed something larger than herself to hold on to but didn't believe in supernatural beings. Her house was the heavy (but not infinitely heavy) and sturdy (but not everlasting) God that she'd loved and served and been sustained by, and my aunt had done a very smart thing by coming when she did.

But now we needed to put the place on the market in a hurry. We were already a week into August, and the house's best selling point, the counterbalance to its many defects (its tiny kitchen, its negligible back yard, its too-small upstairs bathroom), was its situation in the Catholic school district attached to the church of Mary, Queen of Peace. Given the quality of the Webster Groves public schools, I didn't understand why a family would pay extra to live in this district in order to then pay further extra for schooling by nuns, but there were a lot of things I didn't understand about being Catholic. According to my mother, Catholic parents from all over St. Louis eagerly awaited listings in the district, and families in Webster Groves had been known to pull up stakes and move just one or two blocks to get inside its boundaries.

Unfortunately, once the school year started, three weeks

from now, young parents wouldn't be so eager. I felt some additional pressure to help my brother Tom, the executor of the estate, to finish his work quickly. I felt a different kind of pressure from my other brother, Bob, who had urged me to remember that we were talking about real money. ("People knock $782,000 down to $770,000 when they're negotiating, they think it's basically the same number," he'd told me. "Well, no, in fact, *it's twelve thousand dollars less.* I don't know about you, but I can think of a lot of things I'd rather do with twelve thousand dollars than give it to the stranger who's buying my house.") But the really serious pressure came from my mother, who, before she died, had made it clear that there was no better way to honor her memory and validate the last decades of her life than to sell the house for a shocking amount of money.

Counting had always been a comfort to her. She wasn't a collector of anything except Danish Christmas china and mint plate blocks of U.S. postage, but she maintained lists of every trip she'd ever taken, every country she'd set foot in, every one of the "Wonderful (*Exceptional*) European Restaurants" she'd eaten in, every operation she'd undergone, and every insurable object in her house and her safe-deposit box. She was a founding member of a penny-ante investment club called Girl Tycoons, whose portfolio's performance she tracked minutely. In the last two years of her life, as her prognosis worsened, she'd paid particular attention to the sale price of other houses in our neighborhood, writing down their location and square footage. On a sheet of paper marked *Real Estate guide for listing property at 83 Webster Woods,* she'd composed a sample advertisement the way someone else might have drafted her own obituary:

Two story solid brick three bedroom center hall colonial home on shaded lot on cul de sac on private street. There are three bedrooms, living room, dining room with bay, main floor den, eat-in kitchen with new G.E. dishwasher, etc. There are two screened porches, two wood-burning fire-places, two car attached garage, security burglary and fire system, hardwood floors throughout and divided basement.

At the bottom of the page, below a list of new appliances and recent home repairs, was her final guess about the house's worth: "1999—Est. value $350,000.00+." This figure was more than ten times what she and my father had paid for the place in 1965. The house not only constituted the bulk of her assets but was by far the most successful investment she'd ever made. I wasn't a ten times happier person than my father, her grandchildren weren't ten times better educated than she was. What else in her life had done even half so well as real estate?

"It'll sell the house!" my father had exclaimed after he built a little half-bathroom in our basement. "It'll sell the house!" my mother had said after she paid a contractor to redo our front walkway in brick. She repeated the phrase so many times that my father lost his temper and began to enumerate the many improvements *he'd* made, including the new half-bathroom, which she evidently thought would *not* sell the house; he wondered aloud why he'd bothered working every weekend for so many years when all it took to "sell the house" was buying a new brick walkway! He refused to have anything to do with the walkway, leaving it to my mother to scrub the moss off the bricks and to chip away gently at the ice in winter. But after he'd spent half a month of Sundays installing decorative moldings in the dining room, mitering and spackling and painting, he and she both stood and admired the finished work and said, over and over, with great satisfaction, "It'll sell the house."

"It'll sell the house."

"It'll sell the house."

Long past midnight, I turned off the lights downstairs and

went up to my bedroom, which Tom and I had shared until he went away to college. My aunt had done some cleaning before she went back to New York, and I had now taken away all the family pictures, and the bedroom looked ready to show to buyers. The dressertops and desktop were clear; the grain of the carpeting was neatly scalloped from my aunt's vacuuming of it; the twin beds had a freshly made look. And so I was startled, when I peeled back my bedspread, to find something on the mattress by my pillow. It was a bundle of postage stamps in little waxed-paper envelopes: my mother's old collection of plate blocks.

The bundle was so radiantly out of place here that the back of my neck began to tingle, as if I might turn around and see my mother still standing in the doorway. She was clearly the person who'd hidden the stamps. She must have done it in July, as she was getting ready to leave the house for the last time. Some years earlier, when I'd asked her if I could have her old plate blocks, she'd said I was welcome to whatever was left when she died. And possibly she was afraid that Bob, who collected stamps, would appropriate the bundle for himself, or possibly she was just checking items off her to-do list. But she'd taken the envelopes from a drawer in the dining room and moved them upstairs to the one place I would most likely be the next person to disturb. Such micromanagerial prescience! The private message that the stamps represented, the complicit wink in her bypassing of Bob, the signal arriving when the sender was dead: it wasn't the intimate look that Faye Dunaway and Warren Beatty exchange in *Bonnie and Clyde* an instant before they're both shot dead, but it was as close to intimate as my mom and I were going to get. Finding the bundle now was like hearing her say, "I'm paying attention to my details. Are you paying attention to yours?"

The three realtors I interviewed the next day were as various as three suitors in a fairy tale. The first was a straw-haired, shiny-skinned woman from Century 21 for whom it appeared to be a struggle to say nice things about the house. Each room came as a fresh disappointment to her and her strongly cologned male associate; they conferred in low voices about "potential" and "additions." My mother was a bartender's daughter who never finished college, and her taste was what she liked to call Traditional, but it seemed to me unlikely that the other houses on Century 21's list were decorated in substantially *better* taste. I was annoyed by the realtor's failure to be charmed by my mother's Parisian watercolors. The realtor, however, was comparing our quaint little kitchen with the hangarlike spaces in newer houses. If I wanted to list with her, she said, she would suggest asking between $340,000 and $360,000.

The second realtor, a handsome woman named Pat who was wearing an elegant summer suit, was the friend of a good family friend of ours and came highly recommended. She was accompanied by her daughter, Kim, who was in business with her. As the two of them moved from room to room, stopping to admire precisely the details that my mother had been proudest of, they seemed to me two avatars of Webster Groves domesticity. It was as if Pat were thinking of buying the house for Kim; as if Kim would soon be Pat's age and, like Pat, would want a house where everything was quiet and the fabrics and furniture were all just right. Child replacing parent, family succeeding family, the cycle of suburban life. We sat down together in the living room.

"This is a lovely, lovely home," Pat said. "Your mother kept it up beautifully. And I think we can get a good price for it, but we have to act fast. I'd suggest listing it at three hundred fifty thousand, putting an ad in the paper on Tuesday, and having an open house next weekend."

"And your commission?"

"Six percent," she said, looking at me steadily. "I know several people who would be very interested right now."

I told her I would let her know by the end of the day.

The third realtor burst into the house an hour later. Her name was Mike, she was a pretty, short-haired blonde about my own age, and she was wearing excellent jeans. Her plate was overfull, she said in a husky voice, she was coming from her third open house of the day, but after I'd phoned her on Friday she'd driven over to see our house and had fallen in love with it from the street, its curb appeal was *fantastic*, she knew she *had* to see the inside, and, wow, just as she suspected—she was moving hungrily from room to room—it was *adorable*, it was *dripping* with charm, she liked it even better from the inside, and she would love love love love love to be the one to get to sell it, in fact if the upstairs bathroom weren't so small she might even go as high as $405,000, this neighborhood was *so* hot, *so* hot—I knew about the Mary, Queen of Peace school district, right?— but even with the problematic bathroom and the regrettably tiny back yard she wouldn't be surprised if the house sold in the three-nineties, *plus* there were other things she could do for me, her basic commission was five and a half percent, but if the buyer's agent was from her group, she could knock that down to five, and if she herself was the buyer's agent she could knock it all the way down to four, my God, she *loved* what my mother had done, she'd known it as soon as she'd seen it from the street, she wanted this house *bad*—"Jon, I want it *bad*," she said, looking me in the eye—and, by the way, just as a matter of fact, not to brag, truly, but she'd been number one in residential real estate in Webster Groves and Kirkwood for three years running.

Mike excited me. The sweat-damp front of her blouse, the way she strode in her jeans. She was flirting with me broadly, admiring the size of my ambitions, comparing them favorably to her own (though hers were not insubstantial), holding my gaze, and talking nonstop in her lovely husky voice. She said she totally got why I wanted to live in New York. She said it was rare that she met somebody who understood, as I obviously did, about *desire*, about *hunger*. She said she'd price the house between $380,000 and $385,000 and hope to start a bidding war. As I sat there, watching her gush, I felt like a Viking.

It shouldn't have been so hard to make the call to Pat, but it was. She seemed to me a mom I had to disappoint, a mom in the way, a nagging conscience. She seemed to know things about me and about the house—realistic things—that I wished she didn't. The look she'd given me when she'd named her commission had been skeptical and appraising, as if any responsible adult could see that she and her daughter were obviously the best agents for the job, but she wasn't sure if I could see it myself.

I waited until 9:30, the last possible minute, before I called her. Just as I'd feared, she didn't hide her surprise and displeasure. Did I mind if she asked who the other realtor was?

I was conscious of the taste and shape of Mike's name as it passed through my mouth.

"Oh," Pat said wearily. "OK."

Mike wouldn't have been my mother's type either, not one bit. I told Pat that the decision had been a very hard one, a really difficult choice, and that I was grateful that she'd come over and sorry that she and I weren't going to be—

"Well, good luck," she said.

After that, I got to make the fun call, the Yes-I'm-free-on-Friday-night call. Mike, at home, confided to me in a low voice, as if to keep her husband from hearing, "Jon, I knew you'd go with me. I felt the connection between us right away." The only slight complication, she said, was that she had long-standing vacation plans with her husband and children. She was leaving town on Friday and wouldn't be able to start showing the house until the very end of the month. "But don't worry," she said.

I grew up in the middle of the country in the middle of the golden age of the American middle class. My parents were originally Minnesotan, moved south to Chicago, where I was born, and finally came to rest in Missouri, the country's cartographic linchpin. As a child, I set great store by the fact that no American state shares a boundary with more states than Missouri does (it and Tennessee are tied with eight) and that its neighbors abut states as farflung as Georgia and Wyoming. The nation's "population center"—whatever cornfield or county-road crossing the most recent census had identified as America's demographic center of gravity—was never more than a few hours' drive from where we lived. Our winters were better than Minnesota's, our summers were better than Florida's. And our town, Webster Groves, was in the middle of this middle. It wasn't as wealthy a suburb as Ladue or Clayton; it wasn't as close to the inner city as Maplewood or as far out as Des Peres; about seven percent of the population was both middle-class and black. Webster Groves was, my mother liked to say, echoing Goldilocks, "just right."

She and my father had met in an evening philosophy class at the University of Minnesota. My father was working for the Great Northern Railroad and auditing the class for fun. My mother was a full-time receptionist in a doctor's office and was slowly accumulating credits for a degree in child development. She began one of her papers, called "My Philosophy," by describing herself as "an average young American girl—average, I say, in that I have interests, doubts, emotions, and likes similar to those of a girl of my age in any American city." But she then confessed to serious doubts about religion ("I believe firmly in the teachings of Christ, in all He represented, but I am not sure of supernaturalism") which revealed her claim of being "average" as something closer to a *wish*. "I cannot see this doubting for the world as a whole," she wrote. "There is a definite need for religion in the lives of man. I say it is right for humanity, but for myself I do not know." Unable to sign on with God and Heaven and the Resurrection, and uncertain about an economic system that had produced the Great Depression, she concluded her paper by naming the one thing she didn't doubt: "I am a firm believer in family life. I feel that the home is the foundation of true happiness in America—much more the foundation than the church or the school can ever be."

All her life, she hated not belonging. Anything that tended to divide us from the rest of the community (her unbelief, my father's sense of superiority) had to be countered with some principle that would draw us back to the middle and help us to fit in. Whenever she talked to me about my future, she stressed that a person's character mattered more than his or her achievements, and that the more abilities a person had, the more he or she owed society. People who impressed her were always "highly able," never "smart" or "talented," or even "hardworking," because people who thought of themselves as "smart" might be vain or selfish or arrogant, whereas people who considered themselves "able" were constantly reminded of their debt to society.

The American society of my childhood was shaped by similar ideals. Nationwide, the distribution of income had never been more equitable and never would be again; company presidents typically took home only forty times more than their lowest-paid worker. In 1965, near the peak of his career, my father was making $17,000 a year (just over twice the national median income) and had three boys in public school; we owned one mid-sized Dodge and one twenty-inch black-and-white TV; my weekly allowance was twenty-five cents, payable on Sunday mornings; a weekend's excitement might consist of the rental of a steam machine to strip off old wallpaper. To liberals, the mid-century was an era of unexamined materialism at home, unabashed imperialism abroad, the denial of opportunity to women and minorities, the rape of the environment, and the malign hegemony of the military-industrial complex. To conservatives, it was an era of collapsing cultural traditions and bloated federal government and confiscatory tax rates and socialistic welfare and retirement schemes. In the middle of the middle, though, as I watched the old wallpaper come off in heavy, skinlike, pulp-smelling masses that reglued themselves to my father's work boots, there was nothing but family and house and neighborhood and church and school and work. I was cocooned in cocoons that were themselves cocooned. I was the late-arriving son to whom my father, who read to me every weeknight, confided his love of the depressive donkey Eeyore in A. A. Milne, and to whom my mother, at bedtime, sang a private lullaby that she'd made up to celebrate my birth. My parents were adversaries and my brothers were rivals, and each of them complained to me about each of the others, but they were all united in finding me amusing, and there was nothing not to love in them.

Need I add that it didn't last? As my parents grew older and my brothers and I fled the center geographically, ending up on the coasts, so the country as a whole has fled the center economically, ending up with a system in which the wealthiest one percent of the population now takes in sixteen percent of total income (up from eight percent in 1975). This is a great time to be an American CEO, a tough time to be the CEO's lowest-paid worker. A great time to be Wal-Mart, a tough time to be in Wal-Mart's way, a great time to be an incumbent extremist, a tough time to be a moderate challenger. Fabulous to be a defense contractor, shitty to be a reservist, excellent to have tenure at Princeton, grueling to be an adjunct at Queens College; outstanding to manage a pension fund, lousy to rely on one; better than ever to be bestselling, harder than ever to be mid-list; phenomenal to win a Texas Hold 'Em tournament, a drag to be a video-poker addict.

On an August afternoon six years after my mother died, while a major American city was being destroyed by a hurricane, I went golfing with my brother-in-law on a funky little mountain course in northern California. It was a tough time to be in New Orleans but a great time to be out West, where the weather was perfect and the Oakland A's, an underpaid team I like to follow, were making their annual late-summer run at first place. My biggest worries of the day were whether I should feel bad about quitting work at three and whether my favorite organic grocery store would have Meyer lemons for the margaritas I wanted to make après golf. Unlike George Bush's crony Michael Brown, who was thinking about his manicure and his dinner reservations that week, I had the excuse of not being the director of the Federal Emergency Management Agency. With every ball I hooked into the woods or topped into a water hazard, my brother-in-law joked, "At least you're not sitting on a roof with no drinking water, waiting for a helicopter to pick you up." Two days later, when I flew back to New York, I worried that Katrina's aftermath might create unpleasant turbulence on my flight, but the ride was unusually smooth, and the weather in the East was warm and cloudless.

Things had been going well for me in the years since my mother's death. Instead of being in debt and living at the mercy of the city's rent-control laws, I now owned a nice apartment on East Eighty-first Street. Walking in the door, after two months in California, I had the sensation of walking into somebody else's apartment. The guy who lived here was apparently a prosperous middle-aged Manhattanite with the sort of life I'd spent my thirties envying from afar, vaguely disdaining, and finally being defeated in my attempts to imagine my way into. How odd that I now had keys to this guy's apartment.

My housesitter had left the place clean and neat. I'd always favored bare floors and minimal furniture—had had my fill of Traditional when I was growing up—and I'd taken very few things from my mother's house after she died. Kitchenware, photo albums, some pillows. A tool chest that my great-grandfather had made. A painting of a ship that could have been the *Dawn Treader*. An assortment of small objects that I held on to out of loyalty to my mother: an onyx banana, a Wedgwood candy dish, a pewter candlesnuffer, a brass niello-handled letter opener, with matching scissors, in a green leather sheath.

Because there were so few things in the apartment, it didn't take me long to figure out that one of them—the pair of scissors from the sheath—had disappeared while I was in California. My reaction was like that of the dragon Smaug in *The Hobbit*, when Smaug realizes that a gold cup is missing from his mountain of precious objects. I flew around and around the apartment, smoke spewing from my nostrils. When I interrogated the housesitter, who said she hadn't seen the scissors, I had to struggle not to bite her head off. I ransacked the place, went through every drawer and cabinet twice. It enraged me that, of all the things that could have disappeared, what I'd lost had been something of my mother's.

I was enraged about the aftermath of Katrina, too. For a while, that September, I couldn't go online, open a newspaper, or even take cash from an ATM without encountering entreaties to aid the hurricane's homeless victims. The fund-raising apparatus was so far-reaching and well orchestrated it seemed quasi-official, like the "Support Our Troops" ribbons that had shown up on half the country's cars overnight. But it seemed to me that helping Katrina's homeless victims ought to be the government's job, not mine. I'd always voted for candidates who wanted to raise my taxes, because I thought paying taxes was patriotic and because my idea of how to be left alone—my libertarian ideal!—was a well-funded, well-managed central government that spared me from having to make a hundred different spending decisions every week. Like, was Katrina as bad as the Pakistan earthquake? As bad as breast cancer? As bad as AIDS in Africa? Not as bad? How much less bad? I wanted my government to figure these things out.

It was true that the Bush tax cuts had put some extra money in my pocket, and that even those of us who hadn't voted for a privatized America were still obliged to be good citizens. But with government abandoning so many of its former responsibilities, there were now hundreds of new causes to contribute to. Bush hadn't just neglected emergency management and flood control; aside from Iraq, there wasn't much he *hadn't* neglected. Why should I pony up for this particular disaster? And why give political succor to people I believed were ruining the country? If the Republicans were so opposed to big government, let them ask their own donors to pony up! It was possible, moreover, that the antitax billionaires and antitax small-business owners who got antitax representatives elected to Congress were all giving generously to the relief effort, but it seemed equally likely that these people whose idea of injustice was getting to keep only $2 million of their $2.8 million annual income, rather than all of it, were secretly counting on the decency of ordinary Americans to help with Katrina: were playing us for suckers. When private donations replaced federal spending, you had no idea who was freeloading and who was pulling twice their weight.

All of which was to say: my impulse toward charity was now fully subordinate to my political rage. And it wasn't as if I was happy to feel so polarized. I *wanted* to be able to write a check, because I wanted to put Katrina's victims out of my mind and get back to enjoying my life, because, as a New Yorker, I felt I had a right to enjoy my life, because I was living in the number-one terrorist target in the Western Hemisphere, the preferred destination of every future lunatic with a portable nuclear device or smallpox dispenser, and because life in New York was liable to go from great to ghastly even faster than it had in New Orleans. I was arguably already pulling my weight as a citizen simply by living with the many new bull's-eyes that George Bush had painted on my back—and on the back of every other New Yorker—by starting his unwinnable war in Iraq, wasting hundreds of billions of dollars that could have been spent fighting real terrorists, galvanizing a new generation of America-hating jihadists, and deepening our dependence on foreign oil. The shame and the danger of being a citizen of a country that the rest of the world identified with Bush: wasn't this enough of a burden?

I'd been back in the city for two weeks, thinking thoughts like these, when I got a mass e-mailing from a Protestant minister named Chip Jahn. I'd known Jahn and his wife in the 1970s, and more recently I'd gone to visit them at their parsonage in rural southern Indiana, where he'd shown me his two churches and his wife had let me ride her horse. The subject header of his e-mail was "Louisiana Mission," which led me to fear another plea for donations. But Jahn was simply reporting on the tractor-trailers that members of his churches had filled with supplies and driven down to Louisiana:

> A couple of women in the congregation said we ought to send a truck south to help with hurricane relief. The Foertschs were willing to donate a truck and Lynn Winkler and Winkler Foods were willing to help get food and water . . .

Our plans grew as pledges came in. (Just over $35,000 in gifts and pledges. Over $12,000 was from St. Peter and Trinity.) We quickly began looking for another truck and drivers. It turned out to be no more difficult to find these than it was to raise the money. Larry and Mary Ann Wetzel were ready with their truck. Phil Liebering would be their second driver . . .

Foertsch's truck had the heavier but shorter trailer, which was loaded with water. Larry's truck had the pallets of food and baby supplies. We bought $500 worth of towels and washcloths and 100 foam sleeping pads at the last minute, because of the great response of pledges. Both were on Thibodaux's wish list. They were happy to see us. The unloading went quickly and they asked if they could use Wetzel's semitrailer to move the clothes to another warehouse, which meant they could move it with a forklift instead of by hand . . .

Reading Jahn's e-mail, I wished, as I would ordinarily never wish, that I belonged to a church in southern Indiana, so that I could have ridden in one of those trucks. It would have been awkward, of course, to sit in a church every Sunday and sing hymns to a God I didn't believe in. And yet: wasn't this exactly what my parents had done on every Sunday of their adult lives? I wondered how I'd got from their world into the apartment of a person I didn't even recognize as myself. Throughout the autumn, whenever my eyes fell on the half-empty leather sheath, the absence of the scissors stabbed me afresh. I simply couldn't believe they'd disappeared. Months after my return, I was still reransacking drawers and closet shelves I'd searched three times already.

• • •

The other house of my childhood was a sprawling, glass-fronted, six-bedroom rich person's retreat on a vast white-sand beach in the Florida Panhandle. In addition to its private Gulf frontage, the house came with free local golf and deep-sea fishing privileges and a refrigerated beer keg that guests were encouraged to make unlimited use of; there was a phone number to call if the keg ever ran dry. We were able to vacation in this house, living like rich people, for six consecutive Augusts, because the railroad my father worked for sometimes bought rail-maintenance equipment from the house's owner. Without informing the owner, my parents also took the liberty of asking along our good friends Kirby and Ellie, their son David, and, one year, their nephew Paul. That there was something not quite right about these arrangements was evident in my parents' annual reminders to Kirby and Ellie that it was *extremely important* that they not arrive at the house early, lest they run into the owner or the owner's agent.

In 1974, after we'd vacationed in the house for five straight years, my father decided that we had to stop accepting the owner's hospitality. He was giving more and more of his business to one of the owner's competitors, an Austrian manufacturer whose equipment my father considered superior to anything being made in the United States. In the late sixties, he'd helped the Austrians break into the American market, and their gratitude to him had been immediate and total. In the fall of 1970, at the company's invitation, he and my mother had taken their first-ever trip to Europe, visiting Austria and the Alps for a week and Sweden and England for another week. I never found out whether the company paid for absolutely everything, including airfare, or whether it paid only for their meals and their nights in top-drawer hotels like the Imperial in Vienna and the Ritz in Paris, and for the Lincoln Continental and its driver, Johann, who chauffeured my parents around three countries and helped them with their shopping, none of which they could have afforded on their own. Their companions for the trip were the company's head of American operations and his wife, Ilse, who, beginning every day at noon, taught them how to eat and drink like Europeans. My mother was in heaven. She kept a diary of restaurants and hotels and scenic attractions—

> Lunch at Hotel Geiger "Berchtesgarden"—*wonderful* food & spectacular atmosphere—Schnapps, sausage (like raw bacon) & brown bread atop mountain—

and if she was aware of certain historical facts behind the scenery, such as Hitler's frequent visits to Berchtesgaden for recreational getaways, she didn't mention it.

My father had had serious qualms about accepting such lavish hospitality from the Austrians, but my mother had worn him down to the point where he agreed to ask his boss, Mr. German, whether he should decline the invitation. (Mr. German had answered, essentially, "Are you kidding me?") In 1974, when my father voiced misgivings about returning to Florida, my mother again wore him down. She pointed out that Kirby and Ellie were expecting our invitation, and she kept repeating the phrase "Just this one last year," until finally, reluctantly, my father signed off on the usual plan.

Kirby and Ellie were good bridge players, and it would have been a dull trip for my parents with only me along. I was a silent, withdrawn presence in the back seat for the two-day drive through Cape Girardeau, Memphis, Hattiesburg, and Gulfport. As we were driving up the road toward the beach house, on an overcast afternoon made darker by an ominous bank of new high-rise condominiums encroaching from the east, I was struck by how unexcited I was to be arriving this year.

I had just turned fifteen and was more interested in my books and my records than in anything on the beach.

We were within sight of the house's driveway when my mother cried, "Oh no! *No!*" My father cried "Damn!" and swerved off the road, pulling to a stop behind a low dune with sea oats on it. He and my mother—I'd never seen anything like it—crouched down in the front seat and peered over the dashboard.

"Damn!" my father said again, angrily.

And then my mother said it, too: "*Damn!*"

It was the first time and the last time I ever heard her swear. Farther up the road, in the driveway, I could see Kirby standing beside the open door of his and Ellie's sedan. He was chatting affably with a man who, I understood without asking, was the owner of the house.

"Damn!" my father said.

"*Damn!*" my mother said.

"Damn! Damn!"

They'd been caught.

Exactly twenty-five years later, the realtor Mike and my brother Tom agreed on an asking price of $382,000 for the house. Over the Labor Day weekend, when we all gathered in St. Louis to hold a memorial service for my mother, Mike dropped in only briefly. She appeared to have forgotten the ardor of our initial meeting—she barely spoke to me now—and she was subdued and deferential with my brothers. She'd finally held an open house a few days earlier, and of the two prospective buyers who'd shown some interest, neither had made an offer.

In the days after the memorial service, as my brothers and I went from room to room and handled things, I came to feel that the house had been my mother's novel, the concrete story she told about herself. She'd started with the cheap, homely department-store boilerplate she'd bought in 1944. She'd added and replaced various passages as funds permitted, re-upholstering sofas and armchairs, accumulating artwork ever less awful than the prints she'd picked up as a twenty-three-year-old, abandoning her original arbitrary color schemes as she discovered and refined the true interior colors that she carried within her like a destiny. She pondered the arrangement of paintings on a wall like a writer pondering commas. She sat in the rooms year after year and asked herself what might suit her even better. What she wanted was for you to come inside and feel embraced and delighted by what she'd made; she was showing you herself, by way of hospitality; she wanted you to want to stay.

Although the furniture in her final draft was sturdy and well made, of good cherry and maple, my brothers and I couldn't make ourselves want what we didn't want; I couldn't prefer her maple nightstand to the scavenged wine crate that I kept by my bed in New York. And yet to walk away and leave her house so fully furnished, so nearly the way she'd always wanted it to look, gave me the same panicked feeling of *waste* that I'd had two months earlier, when I'd left her still-whole body, with her hands and her eyes and her lips and her skin so perfectly intact and lately functional, for a mortician's helpers to take away and burn.

In October, we hired an estate liquidator to put a price tag on all the things we'd left behind. At the end of the month, people came and bought, and Tom got a check for fifteen thousand dollars, and the liquidator made whatever she hadn't sold just disappear, and I tried not to think about the sad little prices that my mother's worldly goods had fetched.

As for the house, we did our best to sell it while it was still furnished. With the school year under way, and with no eager young Catholic parents bombarding us with offers, we dropped the price to $369,000. A month later, as the estate sale loomed and the oak leaves were coming down, we cut the price again, to $359,000. At Mike's suggestion, we also ran a newspaper ad that showed the house under a Yuletide mantle of snow, looking the way my mother had most liked to see it pictured, along with a new tag line (also a suggestion of Mike's): HOME FOR THE HOL-IDAYS. Nobody went for it. The house stood empty through all of November. None of the things my parents had thought would sell the house had sold it. It was early December before a young couple came along and mercifully offered us $310,000.

By then I was convinced that the realtor Pat could have sold the house in mid-August for my mother's suggested price. My mother would have been stricken to learn how much less we took for it—would have experienced the devaluation as a dashing of her hopes, a rejection of her creative work, an unwelcome indication of her averageness. But this wasn't the big way I'd let her down. She was dead now, after all. She was safely beyond being stricken. What lived on—in me—was the discomfort of how completely I'd outgrown the novel I'd once been so happy to live in, and how little I even cared about the final sale price.

Our friend Kirby, it turned out, had charmed the owner of the Florida house, and the beer keg was fully operational, and so our last week of living like rich people unfolded amicably. I spent morbid, delicious amounts of time by myself, driven by the sort of hormonal instinct that I imagine leads cats to eat grass. The half-finished high-rises to our east were poised to engulf our idyll, even if we'd wanted to come back another year, but the transformation of a quiet, sandpiper-friendly beach into a high-density population center was such a novelty for us that we didn't even have a category for the loss it represented. I studied the skeletal towers the way I studied bad weather.

At the end of the week, my parents and I drove deeper into Florida, so that I could be taken to Disney World. My father was big on fairness, and because my brothers had once spent a day at Disneyland, many years earlier, it was unthinkable that I not be given the equivalent treat of a day at Disney World, whether or not I was too old for it, and whether or not I wanted to be there. I might not have minded going with my friend Manley, or with my not-girlfriend Hoener, and mocking and subverting the place and allowing myself to like it that way. But mocking and subverting in the presence of my parents was out of the question.

In our hotel room in Orlando, I begged my mother to let me wear my cutoff jeans and a T-shirt for the day, but my mother won the argument, and I arrived at Disney World in an ensemble of pleated shorts and a Bing Crosbyish sport shirt. Dressed like this, miserable with self-consciousness, I moved my feet only when I was directly ordered to. All I wanted to do was go sit in our car and read. In front of each themed ride, my mother asked me if it didn't look like lots of fun, but I saw the other teenagers waiting in line, and I felt their eyes on my clothes and my parents, and my throat ached, and I said the line was too long. My mother tried to cajole me, but my father cut her off: "Irene, he doesn't want to ride this one." We trudged on through diffuse, burning Florida sunshine to the next crowded ride. Where, again, the same story.

"You have to ride *something*," my father said finally, after we'd had lunch. We were standing in the lee of an eatery while tawny-legged tourist girls thronged toward the water rides. My eyes fell on a nearby merry-go-round that was empty except for a few toddlers.

"I'll ride that," I said in a dull voice.

For the next twenty minutes, the three of us boarded and re-boarded the dismal merry-go-round, ensuring that our ride tickets weren't going to waste. I stared at the merry-go-round's chevroned metal floor and radiated shame, mentally vomiting back the treat they'd tried to give me. My mother, ever the dutiful traveler, took pictures of my father and me on our uncomfortably small horses, but beneath her forcible cheer she was angry at me, because she knew she was the one I was getting even with, because of our fight about clothes. My father, his fingers loosely grasping a horse-impaling metal pole, gazed into the distance with a look of resignation that summarized his life. I don't see how either of them bore it. I'd been their late, happy child, and now there was nothing I wanted more than to get away from them. My mother seemed to me hideously conformist and hopelessly obsessed with money and appearances; my father seemed to me allergic to every kind of fun. I didn't want the things they wanted. I didn't value what they valued. And we were all equally sorry to be riding the merry-go-round, and we were all equally at a loss to explain what had happened to us.

TWO PONIES

IN MAY 1970, a few nights after National Guardsmen killed four student protesters at Kent State University, my father and my brother Tom started fighting. They weren't fighting about the Vietnam War, which both of them opposed. The fight was probably about a lot of different things at once. But the immediate issue was Tom's summer job. He was a good artist, with a meticulous nature, and my father had encouraged him (you could even say forced him) to choose a college from a short list of schools with strong programs in architecture. Tom had deliberately chosen the most distant of these schools, Rice University, and he'd just returned from his second year in Houston, where his adventures in late-sixties youth culture were pushing him toward majoring in film studies, not architecture. My father, however, had found him a plum summer job with Sverdrup & Parcel, the big engineering firm in St. Louis, whose senior partner, General Leif Sverdrup, had been an Army Corps of Engineers hero in the Philippines. It couldn't have been easy for my father, who was shy about asking favors, to pull the requisite strings at Sverdrup. But the office gestalt was hawkish and buzz-cut and generally inimical to bell-bottomed, lefty film-studies majors; and Tom didn't want to be there.

Up in the bedroom that he and I shared, the windows were open and the air had the stuffy wooden house smell that came out every spring. I preferred the make-believe no-smell of air-conditioning, but my mother, whose subjective experience of temperature was notably consistent with low gas and electricity bills, claimed to be a devotee of "fresh air," and the windows often stayed open until Memorial Day.

On my night table was the *Peanuts Treasury*, a large, thick hardcover compilation of daily and Sunday funnies by Charles M. Schulz. My mother had given it to me the previous Christmas, and I'd been rereading it at bedtime ever since. Like most of the nation's ten-year-olds, I had a private, intense relationship with Snoopy, the cartoon beagle. He was a solitary not-animal animal who lived among larger creatures of a different species, which was more or less my feeling in my own house. My brothers were less like siblings than like an extra, fun pair of quasi-parents. Although I had friends and was a Cub Scout in good standing, I spent a lot of time alone with talking animals. I was an obsessive rereader of A. A. Milne and the Narnia and Dr. Dolittle novels, and my involvement with my collection of stuffed animals was on the verge of becoming age-inappropriate. It was another point of kinship with Snoopy that he, too, liked animal games. He impersonated tigers and vultures and mountain lions, sharks, sea monsters, pythons, cows, piranhas, penguins, and vampire bats. He was the perfect sunny egoist, starring in his ridiculous fantasies and basking in everyone's attention. In a cartoon strip full of children, the dog was the character I recognized as a child.

Tom and my father had been talking in the living room when I went up to bed. Now, at some late and even stuffier hour, after I'd put aside the *Peanuts Treasury* and fallen asleep, Tom burst into our bedroom. He was shouting sarcastically. "You'll get over it! You'll forget about me! It'll be so much easier! You'll get over it!"

My father was offstage somewhere, making large abstract sounds. My mother was right behind Tom, sobbing at his shoulder, begging him to stop, to stop. He was pulling open dresser drawers, repacking bags he'd only recently unpacked. "You think you want me here," he said, "but you'll get over it."

What about me? my mother pleaded. *What about Jon?*

"You'll get over it."

I was a small and fundamentally ridiculous person. Even if I'd dared sit up in bed, what could I have said? "Excuse me, I'm trying to sleep"? I lay still and followed the action through my eyelashes. There were further dramatic comings and goings, through some of which I may in fact have slept. Finally I heard Tom's feet pounding down the stairs and my mother's terrible cries, now nearly shrieks, receding after him: "Tom! Tom! Tom! Please! Tom!" And then the front door slammed.

Things like this had never happened in our house. The worst fight I'd ever witnessed was between my brothers on the subject of Frank Zappa, whose music Tom admired and Bob one afternoon dismissed with such patronizing disdain that Tom began to sneer at Bob's own favorite group, the Supremes; which led to bitter words. But a scene of real wailing and open rage was completely off the map. When I woke up the next morning, the memory of it already felt decades old and semi-dreamlike and unmentionable.

My father had left for work, and my mother served me breakfast without comment. The food on the table, the jingles on the radio, and the walk to school all were unremarkable; and yet everything about the day was soaked in dread. At school that week, in Miss Niblack's class, we were rehearsing our fifth-grade play. The script, which I'd written, had a large number of bit parts and one very generous role that I'd created with my own memorization abilities in mind. The action took place on a boat, involved a taciturn villain named Mr. Scuba, and lacked the most rudimentary comedy, point, or moral. Not even I, who got to do most of the talking, enjoyed being in it. Its badness—my responsibility for its badness—became part of the day's general dread.

There was something dreadful about springtime itself. The riot of biology, the *Lord of the Flies* buzzing, the pullulating mud. After school, instead of staying outside to play, I followed my dread home and cornered my mother in our dining room. I asked her about my upcoming class performance. Would Dad be in town for it? What about Bob? Would Bob be home from college yet? And what about Tom? Would Tom be there, too? This was quite plausibly an innocent line of questioning—I was a small glutton for attention, forever turning conversations to the subject of myself—and, for a while, my mother gave me plausibly innocent answers. Then she slumped into a chair, put her face in her hands, and began to weep.

"Didn't you hear anything last night?" she said.

"No."

"You didn't hear Tom and Dad shouting? You didn't hear doors slamming?"

"No!"

She gathered me in her arms, which was probably the main thing I'd been dreading. I stood there stiffly while she hugged me. "Tom and Dad had a terrible fight," she said. "After you went to bed. They had a terrible fight, and Tom got his things and left the house, and we don't know where he went."

"Oh."

"I thought we'd hear from him today, but he hasn't called, and I'm frantic, not knowing where he is. I'm just frantic!"

I squirmed a little in her grip.

"But this has nothing to do with you," she said. "It's between him and Dad and has nothing to do with you. I'm sure Tom's sorry he won't be here to see your play. Or maybe, who knows, he'll be back by Friday and he will see it."

"OK."

"But I don't want you telling anyone he's gone until we know where he is. Will you agree not to tell anyone?"

"OK," I said, breaking free of her. "Can we turn the air-conditioning on?"

I was unaware of it, but an epidemic had broken out across the country. Late adolescents in suburbs like ours had suddenly gone berserk, running away to other cities to have sex and not go to college, ingesting every substance they could get their hands on, not just clashing with their parents but rejecting and annihilating everything about them. For a while, the parents were so frightened and so mystified and so ashamed that each family, especially mine, quarantined itself and suffered by itself.

When I went upstairs, my bedroom felt like an overwarm sickroom. The clearest remaining vestige of Tom was the *Don't Look Back* poster that he'd taped to a flank of his dresser where Bob Dylan's psychedelic hairstyle wouldn't always be catching my mother's censorious eye. Tom's bed, neatly made, was the bed of a kid carried off by an epidemic.

In that unsettled season, as the so-called generation gap was rending the cultural landscape, Charles Schulz's work was uniquely beloved. Fifty-five million Americans had seen *A Charlie Brown Christmas* the previous December, for a Nielsen share of better than fifty percent. The musical *You're a Good Man, Charlie Brown* was in its second sold-out year on Broadway. The astronauts of Apollo X, in their dress rehearsal of the first lunar landing, had christened their orbiter and landing vehicle *Charlie Brown* and *Snoopy*. Newspapers carrying "Peanuts" reached more than 150 million readers, "Peanuts" collections were all over the bestseller lists, and if my own friends were any indication, there was hardly a kid's bedroom in America without a "Peanuts" wastebasket or "Peanuts" bedsheets or a "Peanuts" wall hanging. Schulz, by a luxurious margin, was the most famous living artist on the planet.

To the countercultural mind, the strip's square panels were the only square thing about it. A begoggled beagle piloting a doghouse and getting shot down by the Red Baron had the same antic valence as Yossarian paddling a dinghy to Sweden. Wouldn't the country be better off listening to Linus Van Pelt than to Robert McNamara? This was the era of flower children, not flower adults. But the strip appealed to older Americans as well. It was unfailingly inoffensive (Snoopy never lifted a leg) and was set in a safe, attractive suburb where the kids, except for Pigpen, whose image Ron McKernan of the Grateful Dead pointedly embraced, were clean and well-spoken and conservatively dressed. Hippies and astronauts, the rejecting kids and the rejected grownups, were all of one mind here.

An exception was my own household. As far as I know, my father never in his life read a comic strip, and my mother's interest in the funnies was limited to a single-panel feature called "The Girls," whose generic middle-aged matrons, with their weight problems and stinginess and poor driving skills and weakness for department-store bargains, she found just endlessly amusing.

I didn't buy comic books, not even *Mad* magazine, but I worshipped at the altars of Warner Bros. cartoons and the funnies section of the *St. Louis Post-Dispatch*. I read the section's black-and-white page first, skipping the dramatic features like "Steve Roper" and "Juliet Jones" and glancing at "Li'l Abner" only to satisfy myself that it was still trashy and repellent. On the full-color back page I read the strips strictly in reverse order of preference, doing my best to be amused by Dagwood Bumstead's midnight snacks and struggling to ignore the fact that Tiger and Punkinhead were the kind of messy, unreflective kids whom I disliked in real life, before I treated myself to my favorite strip, "B.C." The strip, by Johnny Hart, was caveman humor. Hart wrung hundreds of gags from the friendship between a flightless bird and a long-suffering tortoise who was constantly attempting unturtlish feats of agility and flexibility. Debts were always paid in clams; dinner was always roast leg of something. When I was done with "B.C.," I was done with the paper.

The comics in St. Louis's other paper, the *Globe-Democrat*, which my parents didn't take, seemed bleak and foreign to me. "Broom Hilda" and "Funky Winkerbean" and "The Family Circus" were off-putting in the manner of the kid whose partially visible underpants, which had the name CUTTAIR handmarkered on the waistband, I'd stared at throughout my family's tour of the Canadian parliament. Although "The Family Circus" was resolutely unfunny, its panels clearly were based on some actual family's humid, baby-filled home life and were aimed at an audience that recognized this life, which compelled me to posit an entire subspecies of humanity that found "The Family Circus" hilarious.

I knew very well, of course, why the *Globe-Democrat*'s cartoons were so lame: the paper that carried "Peanuts" didn't *need* any other good strips. Indeed, I would have swapped the entire *Post-Dispatch* for a daily dose of Schulz. Only "Peanuts," the strip we didn't get, dealt with stuff that really mattered. I didn't for a minute believe that the children in "Peanuts" were really children—they were so much more emphatic and cartoonishly *real* than anybody in my own neighborhood—but I nevertheless took their stories to be dispatches from a universe of childhood more substantial and convincing than my own. Instead of playing kickball and Four Square, the way my friends and I did, the kids in "Peanuts" had real baseball teams, real football equipment, real fistfights. Their relationships with Snoopy were far richer than the chasings and bitings that constituted my own relationships with neighborhood dogs. Minor but incredible disasters, often involving new vocabulary words, befell them daily. Lucy was "blackballed by the Bluebirds." She knocked Charlie Brown's croquet ball so far that he had to call the other players from a phone booth. She gave Charlie Brown a signed document in which she swore not to pull the football away when he tried to kick it, but the "peculiar thing about this document," as she observed in the final frame, was that "it was never notarized." When Lucy smashed the bust of Beethoven on Schroeder's toy piano, it struck me as odd and funny that Schroeder had a closet full of identical replacement busts, but I accepted it as humanly possible, because Schulz had drawn it.

To the *Peanuts Treasury* I soon added two other equally strong hardcover collections, *Peanuts Revisited* and *Peanuts Classics*. A well-meaning relative once also gave me a copy of Robert Short's bestseller, *The Gospel According to Peanuts*, but it couldn't have interested me less. "Peanuts" wasn't a portal on the Gospel. It was my gospel.

Chapter 1, verses 1–4, of what I knew about disillusionment: Charlie Brown passes the house of the Little Red-Haired Girl, the object of his eternal fruitless longing. He sits down with Snoopy and says, "I wish I had two ponies." He imagines offering one of the ponies to the Little Red-Haired Girl, riding out into the countryside with her, and sitting down with her beneath a tree. Suddenly he's scowling at Snoopy and asking, "Why aren't you two ponies?" Snoopy, rolling his eyes, thinks: "I knew we'd get around to that."

Or Chapter 1, verses 26–32, of what I knew about the mysteries of etiquette: Linus is showing off his new wristwatch to everyone in the neighborhood. "New watch!" he says proudly to Snoopy, who, after a hesitation, licks it. Linus's hair stands on end. "YOU LICKED MY WATCH!" he cries. "It'll rust! It'll turn green! He ruined it!" Snoopy is left looking mildly puzzled and thinking, "I thought it would have been impolite not to taste it."

Or Chapter 2, verses 6–12, of what I knew about fiction: Linus is annoying Lucy, wheedling and pleading with her to read him a story. To shut him up, she grabs a book, randomly opens it, and says, "A man was born, he lived and he died. The End!" She tosses the book aside, and Linus picks it up reverently. "What a fascinating account," he says. "It almost makes you wish you had known the fellow."

The perfect silliness of stuff like this, the koanlike inscrutability, entranced me even when I was ten. But many of the more elaborate sequences, especially the ones about Charlie Brown's humiliation and loneliness, made only a generic impression on me. In a classroom spelling bee that Charlie Brown has been looking forward to, the first word he's asked to spell is "maze." With a complacent smile, he produces "M-A-Y-S." The class screams with laughter. He returns to his seat and presses his face into his desktop, and when his teacher asks him what's wrong, he yells at her and ends up in the principal's office. "Peanuts" was steeped in Schulz's awareness that for every winner in a competition there has to be a loser, if not twenty losers, or two thousand, but I personally enjoyed winning and couldn't see why so much fuss was made about the losers.

In the spring of 1970, Miss Niblack's class was studying homonyms to prepare for what she called the Homonym Spelldown. I did some desultory homonym drilling with my mother, rattling off "sleigh" for "slay" and "slough" for "slew" the way other kids roped softballs into center field. To me, the only halfway interesting question about the Spelldown was who was going to come in second. A new kid had joined our class that year, a shrimpy black-haired striver, Chris Toczko, who had it in his head that he and I were academic rivals. I was a nice enough little boy as long as you kept away from my turf. Toczko was annoyingly unaware that I, not he, by natural right, was the best student in the class. On the day of the Spelldown, he actually taunted me. He said he'd done a lot of studying and he was going to beat me! I looked down at the little pest and did not know what to say. I evidently mattered a lot more to him than he did to me.

For the Spelldown, we all stood by the blackboard, Miss Niblack calling out one half of a pair of homonyms and my classmates sitting down as soon as they had failed. Toczko was pale and trembling, but he knew his homonyms. He was the last kid standing, besides me, when Miss Niblack called out the word "liar." Toczko trembled and essayed: "L . . . I . . ." And I could see that I had beaten him. I waited impatiently while, with considerable anguish, he extracted two more letters from his marrow: "E . . . R?"

"I'm sorry, Chris, that's not a word," Miss Niblack said.

With a sharp laugh of triumph, not even waiting for Toczko to sit down, I stepped forward and sang out, "L-Y-R-E! *Lyre*. It's a stringed instrument."

I hadn't really doubted that I would win, but Toczko had got to me with his taunting, and my blood was up. I was the last person in class to realize that Toczko was having a meltdown. His face turned red and he began to cry, insisting angrily that "lier" *was* a word, it *was* a word.

I didn't care if it was a word or not. I knew my rights. However many homonyms of "liar" might exist in theory, the word Miss Niblack wanted was clearly "lyre." Toczko's tears disturbed and disappointed me, as I made quite clear by fetching the classroom dictionary and showing him that "lier" wasn't in it. This was how both Toczko and I ended up in the principal's office.

I'd never been sent down before. I was interested to learn that the principal, Mr. Barnett, had a Webster's International Unabridged in his office. Toczko, who barely outweighed the dictionary, used two hands to open it and to roll back the pages to the "L" words. I stood at his shoulder and saw where his tiny, trembling index finger was pointing: *lier, n., one that lies (as in ambush)*. Mr. Barnett immediately declared us co-winners of the Spelldown—a compromise that didn't seem quite fair to me, since I would surely have murdered Toczko if we'd gone another round. But his outburst had spooked me, and I decided it might be OK, for once, to let somebody else win.

A few months after the Homonym Spelldown, just after summer vacation started, Toczko ran out into Grant Road and was killed by a car. What little I knew then about the world's badness I knew mainly from a camping trip, some years earlier, when I'd dropped a frog into a campfire and watched it shrivel and roll down the flat side of a log. My memory of that shriveling and rolling was sui generis, distinct from my other memories. It was like a nagging, sick-making atom of rebuke in me. I felt similarly rebuked now when my mother, who knew nothing of Toczko's rivalry with me, told me that he was dead. She was weeping as she'd wept over Tom's disappearance some weeks earlier. She sat me down and made me write a letter of condolence to Toczko's mother. I was very much unaccustomed to considering the interior states of people other than myself, but it was impossible not to consider Mrs. Toczko's. Though I never met her in person, in the ensuing weeks I pictured her suffering so incessantly and vividly that I could almost see her: a tiny, trim, dark-haired woman who cried the way her son did.

. . .

"Everything I do makes me feel guilty," says Charlie Brown. He's at the beach, and he has just thrown a pebble into the water, and Linus has commented, "Nice going . . . It took that rock four thousand years to get to shore, and now you've thrown it back."

I felt guilty about Toczko. I felt guilty about the little frog. I felt guilty about shunning my mother's hugs when she seemed to need them most. I felt guilty about the washcloths at the bottom of the stack in the linen closet, the older, thinner washcloths that we seldom used. I felt guilty for preferring my best shooter marbles, a solid red agate and a solid yellow agate, my king and my queen, to marbles farther down my rigid marble hierarchy. I felt guilty about the board games that I didn't like to play—Uncle Wiggily, U.S. Presidential Elections, Game of the States—and sometimes, when my friends weren't around, I opened the boxes and examined the pieces in the hope of making the games feel less forgotten. I felt guilty about neglecting the stiff-limbed, scratchy-pelted Mr. Bear, who had no voice and didn't mix well with my other stuffed animals. To avoid feeling guilty about them, too, I slept with one of them per night, according to a strict weekly schedule.

We laugh at dachshunds for humping our legs, but our own species is even more self-centered in its imaginings. There's no object so Other that it can't be anthropomorphized and shanghaied into conversation with us. Some objects are more amenable than others, however. The trouble with Mr. Bear was that he was more realistically bearlike than the other animals. He had a distinct, stern, feral persona; unlike our faceless washcloths, he was assertively Other. It was no wonder I couldn't speak through him. An old shoe is easier to invest with comic personality than is, say, a photograph of Cary Grant. The blanker the slate, the more easily we can fill it with our own image.

Our visual cortexes are wired to quickly recognize faces and then quickly subtract massive amounts of detail from them, zeroing in on their essential message: Is this person happy? Angry? Fearful? Individual faces may vary greatly, but a smirk on one is a lot like a smirk on another. Smirks are conceptual, not pictorial. Our brains are like cartoonists—and cartoonists are like our brains, simplifying and exaggerating, subordinating facial detail to abstract comic concepts.

Scott McCloud, in his cartoon treatise *Understanding Comics*, argues that the image you have of yourself when you're conversing is very different from your image of the person you're conversing with. Your interlocutor may produce universal smiles and universal frowns, and they may help you to identify with him emotionally, but he also has a particular nose and particular skin and particular hair that continually remind you that he's an Other. The image you have of your own face, by contrast, is highly cartoonish. When you feel yourself smile, you imagine a cartoon of smiling, not the complete skin-and-nose-and-hair package. It's precisely the simplicity and universality of cartoon faces, the absence of Otherly particulars, that invite us to love them as we love ourselves. The most widely loved (and profitable) faces in the modern world tend to be exceptionally basic and abstract cartoons: Mickey Mouse, the Simpsons, Tintin, and—simplest of all, barely more than a circle, two dots, and a horizontal line—Charlie Brown.

Charles Schulz only ever wanted to be a cartoonist. He was born in St. Paul in 1922, the only child of a German father and a mother of Norwegian extraction. Much of the existing Schulzian literature dwells on the Charlie Brownish traumas in his early life: his skinniness and pimples, his unpopularity with girls at school, the inexplicable rejection of a batch of his drawings by his high-school yearbook, and, some years later, the rejection of his marriage proposal by the real-life Little Red-Haired Girl, Donna Mae Johnson. Schulz himself spoke of his youth in a tone close to anger. "It took me a long time to become a human being," he told an interviewer in 1987.

> I was regarded by many as kind of sissyfied, which I resented because I really was not a sissy. I was not a tough guy, but . . . I was good at any sport where you threw things, or hit them, or caught them, or something like that. I hated things like swimming and tumbling and those kinds of things, so I was really not a sissy. [. . . But] the coaches were so intolerant and there was no program for all of us. So I never regarded myself as being much and I never regarded myself as good looking and I never had a date in high school, because I thought, who'd want to date me? So I didn't bother.

Schulz "didn't bother" going to art school, either—it would only have discouraged him, he said, to be around people who could draw better than he could.

On the eve of Schulz's induction into the Army, his mother died of cancer. Schulz later described the loss as a catastrophe from which he almost did not recover. During basic training he was depressed, withdrawn, and grieving. In the long run, though, the Army was good for him. He entered the service, he recalled later, as a "nothing person" and came out as a staff sergeant in charge of a machine-gun squadron. "I thought, by golly, if that isn't a man, I don't know what is," he said. "And I felt good about myself, and that lasted about eight minutes, and then I went back to where I am now."

After the war, he returned to his childhood neighborhood, lived with his father, became intensely involved in a Christian youth group, and learned to draw kids. For the rest of his life, he virtually never drew adults. He avoided adult vices—didn't drink, didn't smoke, didn't swear—and, in his work, he spent more and more time in the imagined yards and sandlots of his childhood. He was childlike, too, in the absoluteness of his scruples and inhibitions. Even after he became famous and powerful, he was reluctant to demand a more flexible layout for "Peanuts," because he didn't think it was fair to the papers that had been his loyal customers. He also thought it was unfair to draw caricatures. ("If somebody has a big nose," he said, "I'm sure that they regret the fact they have a big nose and who am I to point it out in gross caricature?") His resentment of the name "Peanuts," which his editors had given the strip in 1950, was still fresh at the end of his life. "To label something that was going to be a life's work with a name like 'Peanuts' was really insulting," he told an interviewer in 1987. To the suggestion that thirty-seven years might have softened the insult, Schulz replied: "No, no. I hold a grudge, boy."

Was Schulz's comic genius the product of his psychic wounds? Certainly the middle-aged artist was a mass of resentments and phobias that seemed attributable, in turn, to early traumas. He was increasingly prone to attacks of depression and bitter loneliness ("Just the mention of a hotel makes me turn cold," he told his biographer), and when he finally broke away from his native Minnesota he set about replicating its comforts in California, building himself an ice rink where the snack bar was called "Warm Puppy." By the 1970s, he was reluctant even to get on an airplane unless someone from his family was with him. This would seem to be a classic instance of the pathology that produces great art: wounded in his adolescence, our hero took permanent refuge in the childhood world of "Peanuts."

But what if Schulz had chosen to become a toy salesman, rather than an artist? Would he still have lived such a withdrawn and emotionally turbulent life? I suspect not. I suspect that Schulz the toy salesman would have gutted his way through a normal life the same way he'd gutted out his military service. He would have done whatever it took to support his family—begged a Valium prescription from his doctor, had a few drinks at the hotel bar.

Schulz wasn't an artist because he suffered. He suffered because he was an artist. To keep choosing art over the comforts of a normal life—to grind out a strip every day for fifty years; to pay the very steep psychic price for this—is the opposite of damaged. It's the sort of choice that only a tower of strength and sanity can make. The reason that Schulz's early sorrows look like "sources" of his later brilliance is that he had the talent and resilience to find humor in them. Almost every young person experiences sorrows. What's distinctive about Schulz's childhood is not his suffering but the fact that he loved comics from an early age, was gifted at drawing, and had the undivided attention of two loving parents.

Every February, Schulz drew a strip about Charlie Brown's failure to get any valentines. Schroeder, in one installment, chides Violet for trying to fob off a discarded valentine on Charlie Brown several days after Valentine's Day, and Charlie Brown shoves Schroeder aside with the words "Don't interfere—I'll take it!" But the story Schulz told about his own childhood experience with valentines was very different. When he was in first grade, he said, his mother helped him make a valentine for each of his classmates, so that nobody would be offended by not getting one, but he felt too shy to put them in the box at the front of the classroom, and so he took them all home again to his mother. At first glance, this story recalls a 1957 strip in which Charlie Brown peers over a fence at a swimming pool full of happy kids and then trudges home by himself and sits in a bucket of water. But Schulz, unlike Charlie Brown, had a mother on duty—a mother to whom he chose to give his entire basket. A child deeply scarred by a failure to get valentines would probably not grow up to draw lovable strips about the pain of never getting valentines. A child like that—one thinks of R. Crumb—might instead draw a valentine box that morphs into a vulva that devours his valentines and then devours him, too.

This is not to say that the depressive and failure-ridden Charlie Brown, the selfish and sadistic Lucy, the philosophizing oddball Linus, and the obsessive Schroeder (whose Beethoven-sized ambitions are realized on a one-octave toy piano) aren't all avatars of Schulz. But his true alter ego is clearly Snoopy: the protean trickster whose freedom is founded on his confidence that he's lovable at heart, the quick-change artist who, for the sheer joy of it, can become a helicopter or a hockey player or Head Beagle and then again, in a flash, before his virtuosity has a chance to alienate you or diminish you, be the eager little dog who just wants dinner.

I never heard my father tell a joke. Sometimes he reminisced about a business colleague who ordered a "Scotch and Coke" and a "flander" fillet in a Dallas diner in July, and he could laugh at his own embarrassments, his impolitic remarks at the office, his foolish mistakes on home-improvement projects; but there wasn't a silly bone in his body. He responded to other people's jokes with a wince or a grimace. As a boy, I told him a story I'd made up about a trash-hauling company cited for "fragrant violations." He shook his head, stone-faced, and said, "Not plausible."

In another archetypical "Peanuts" strip, Violet and Patty are abusing Charlie Brown in vicious stereo: "GO ON HOME! WE DON'T WANT YOU AROUND HERE!" He trudges away with his eyes on the ground, and Violet remarks, "It's a strange thing about Charlie Brown. You almost never see him laugh."

The few times he ever played catch with me, my father threw the ball like a thing he wanted to get rid of, a piece of rotten fruit, and he snatched at my return throws with an awkward pawing motion. I never saw him touch a football or a Frisbee. His two main recreations were golf and bridge, and his enjoyment of them consisted in perpetually reconfirming that he was useless at the one and unlucky at the other.

He only ever wanted not to be a child anymore. His parents were a pair of nineteenth-century Scandinavians caught up in a Hobbesian struggle to prevail in the swamps of north-central Minnesota. His popular, charismatic older brother drowned in a hunting accident when he was still a young man. His nutty and pretty and spoiled younger sister had an only daughter who died in a one-car accident when she was twenty-two. My father's parents also died in a one-car accident, but only after regaling him with prohibitions, demands, and criticisms for fifty years. He never said a harsh word about them. He never said a nice word, either.

The few childhood stories he told were about his dog, Spider, and his gang of friends in the invitingly named little town, Palisade, that his father and uncles had constructed among the swamps. The local high school was eight miles from Palisade. In order to attend, my father lived in a boardinghouse for a year and later commuted in his father's Model A. He was a social cipher, invisible after school. The most popular girl in his class, Romelle Erickson, was expected to be the valedictorian, and the school's "social crowd" was "shocked," my father told me many times, when it turned out that the "country boy," "Earl Who," had claimed the title.

When he registered at the University of Minnesota, in 1933, his father went with him and announced, at the head of the registration line, "He's going to be a civil engineer." For the rest of his life, my father was restless. In his thirties, he agonized about whether to study medicine; in his forties, he was offered a partnership in a contracting firm which, to my mother's ever-lasting disappointment, he wasn't bold enough to accept; in his fifties and sixties, he admonished me never to let a corporation exploit my talents. In the end, though, he spent fifty years doing exactly what his father had told him to do.

After he died, I came into a few boxes of his papers. Most of the stuff was disappointingly unrevealing, and from his early childhood there was nothing except one brown envelope in which he'd saved a thick bundle of valentines. Some of them were flimsy and unsigned, some of them were more elaborate, with crepe-paper solids or 3-D foldouts, and a few from "Margaret" were in actual envelopes; the styles ranged from backwoods Victorian to 1920s art deco. The signatures—most of them from the boys and girls his age, a few from his cousins, one from his sister—were in the crude handwriting of elementary school. The gushiest profusions came from his best friend, Walter Anderson. But there weren't any valentines from his parents, or any other cards or tokens of their love, in any of the boxes.

My mother called him "oversensitive." She meant that it was easy to hurt his feelings, but the sensitivity was physical as well. When he was young, a doctor gave him a pinprick test that showed him to be allergic to "almost everything," including wheat, milk, and tomatoes. A different doctor, whose office was at the top of five long flights of stairs, greeted him with a blood-pressure test and immediately declared him unfit to fight the Nazis. Or so my father told me, with a shrugging gesture and an odd smile (as if to say, "What could I do?"), when I asked him why he hadn't been in the war. Even as a teenager, I sensed that his social awkwardness and sensitivities had been aggravated by not serving. He came from a family of pacifist Swedes, however, and was very happy not to be a soldier. He was happy that my brothers had college deferments and good luck with the lottery. Among his war-vet colleagues, he was such an outlier on the subject of Vietnam that he didn't dare talk about it. At home, in private, he aggressively avowed that, if Tom had drawn a bad number, he personally would have driven him to Canada.

Tom was a second-born in the mold of my father. He got poison ivy so bad it was like measles. He had a mid-October birthday and was perennially the youngest kid in his classes. On his only date in high school, he was so nervous that he forgot his baseball tickets and left the car idling in the street while he ran back inside; the car rolled down the hill and punched through an asphalt curb, clearing two levels of a terraced garden, and came to rest on a neighbor's front lawn.

To me, it simply added to Tom's mystique that the car was not only still drivable but entirely undamaged. Neither he nor Bob could do any wrong in my eyes. They were expert whistlers and chess players, amazing wielders of tools and pencils, and the sole suppliers of whatever anecdotes and data I was able to impress my friends with. In the margins of Tom's school copy of *A Portrait of the Artist as a Young Man*, he drew a two-hundred-page riffle-animation of a stick-figure pole-vaulter clearing a hurdle, landing on his head, and being carted away on a stretcher by stick-figure E.M.S. personnel. This seemed to me a masterwork of filmic art and science. But my father had told Tom: "You'd make a good architect, here are three schools to choose from." He said: "You're going to work for Sverdrup."

Tom was gone for five days before we heard from him. His call came on a Sunday after church. We were sitting on the screen porch, and my mother ran the length of the house to answer the phone. She sounded so ecstatic with relief I felt embarrassed for her. Tom had hitchhiked back to Houston and was doing deep-fry at a Church's fried-chicken establishment, hoping to save enough money to join his best friend in Colorado. My mother kept asking him when he might come home, assuring him that he was welcome and that he wouldn't have to work at Sverdrup; but I could tell, without even hearing Tom's responses, that he wanted nothing to do with us now.

The purpose of a comic strip, Schulz liked to say, was to sell newspapers and to make people laugh. His formulation may look self-deprecating at first glance, but in fact it is an oath of loyalty. When I. B. Singer, in his Nobel address, declared that the novelist's first responsibility is to be a storyteller, he didn't say "mere storyteller," and Schulz didn't say "merely make people laugh." He was loyal to the reader who wanted something funny from the funny pages. Just about anything—protesting against world hunger; getting a laugh out of words like "nooky"; dispensing wisdom; dying—is easier than real comedy.

Schulz never stopped trying to be funny. Around 1970, though, he began to drift away from aggressive humor and into melancholy reverie. There came tedious meanderings in Snoopyland with the unhilarious bird Woodstock and the unamusing beagle Spike. Certain leaden devices, such as Marcie's insistence on calling Peppermint Patty "sir," were heavily recycled. By the late eighties, the strip had grown so quiet that younger friends of mine seemed baffled by my fandom. It didn't help that later "Peanuts" anthologies loyally reprinted so many Spike and Marcie strips. The volumes that properly showcased Schulz's genius, the three hardcover collections from the sixties, had gone out of print.

Still more harmful to Schulz's reputation were his own

kitschy spinoffs. Even in the sixties, you had to fight through cloying Warm Puppy paraphernalia to reach the comedy; the cuteness levels in latter-day "Peanuts" TV specials tied my toes in knots. What first made "Peanuts" "Peanuts" was cruelty and failure, and yet every "Peanuts" greeting card and tchotchke and blimp had to feature somebody's sweet, crumpled smile. Everything about the billion-dollar "Peanuts" industry argued against Schulz as an artist to be taken seriously. Far more than Disney, whose studios were churning out kitsch from the start, Schulz came to seem an icon of art's corruption by commerce, which sooner or later paints a smiling sales face on everything it touches. The fan who wants to see him as an artist sees a merchant instead. Why isn't he two ponies?

It's hard to repudiate a comic strip, however, if your memories of it are more vivid than your memories of your own life. When Charlie Brown went off to summer camp, I went along in my imagination. I heard him trying to make conversation with the fellow camper who lay in his bunk and refused to say anything but "Shut up and leave me alone." I watched when he finally came home again and shouted to Lucy, "I'm back! I'm back!" and Lucy gave him a bored look and said, "Have you been away?"

I went to camp myself, in the summer of 1970. But aside from an alarming personal hygiene situation which seemed to have resulted from my peeing in some poison ivy, and which, for several days, I was convinced was either a fatal tumor or puberty, my camp experience paled beside Charlie Brown's. The best part of it was coming home and seeing Bob waiting for me, in his new Karmann Ghia, at the YMCA parking lot.

Tom was also home by then. He'd managed to make his way to his friend's house in Colorado, but the friend's parents weren't happy about harboring somebody else's runaway son, and so they'd sent Tom back to St. Louis. Officially, I was very excited that he was back. In truth, I was embarrassed to be around him. I was afraid that if I referred to his sickness and our quarantine I might prompt a relapse. I wanted to live in a "Peanuts" world where rage was funny and insecurity was lovable. The littlest kid in my "Peanuts" books, Sally Brown, grew older for a while and then hit a glass ceiling and went no further. I wanted everyone in my family to get along and nothing to change; but suddenly, after Tom ran away, it was as if the five of us looked around, asked why we should be spending time together, and failed to come up with many good answers.

For the first time, in the months that followed, my parents' conflicts became audible. My father came home on cool nights to complain about the house's "chill." My mother countered that the house wasn't cold if you were *doing housework all day*. My father marched into the dining room to adjust the thermostat and dramatically point to its "Comfort Zone," a pale-blue arc between 72 and 78 degrees. My mother said that she was *so hot*. And I decided, as always, not to voice my suspicion that the Comfort Zone referred to air-conditioning in the summer rather than heat in the winter. My father set the temperature at 72 and retreated to the den, which was situated directly above the furnace. There was then a lull, and then big explosions. No matter what corner of the house I hid myself in, I could hear my father bellowing, "LEAVE THE GOD-DAMNED THERMOSTAT ALONE!"

"Earl, I didn't touch it!"

"You did! Again!"

"I didn't think I even moved it, I just *looked* at it, I didn't mean to change it."

"Again! You monkeyed with it again! I had it set where I wanted it. And you moved it down to seventy!"

"Well, if I did somehow change it, I'm sure I didn't mean to. You'd be hot, too, if you worked all day in the kitchen."

"All I ask at the end of a long day at work is that the temperature be set in the Comfort Zone."

"Earl, it is so hot in the kitchen. You don't know, because you're never *in* here, but it is *so* hot."

"The *low end* of the Comfort Zone! Not even the middle! The low end! It is not too much to ask!"

And I wonder why "cartoonish" remains such a pejorative. It took me half my life to achieve seeing my parents as cartoons. And to become more perfectly a cartoon myself: what a victory that would be.

My father eventually applied technology to the problem of temperature. He bought a space heater to put behind his chair in the dining room, where he was bothered in winter by drafts from the bay window behind him. Like so many of his appliance purchases, the heater was a pathetically cheap little thing, a wattage hog with a stertorous fan and a grinning orange mouth which dimmed the lights and drowned out conversation and produced a burning smell every time it cycled on. When I was in high school, he bought a quieter, more expensive model. One evening my mother and I started reminiscing about the old model, caricaturing my father's temperature sensitivities, doing cartoons of the little heater's faults, the smoke and the buzzing, and my father got mad and left the table. He thought we were ganging up on him. He thought I was being cruel, and I was, but I was also forgiving him.

THEN JOY BREAKS THROUGH

WE MET ON Sundays at five-thirty. We chose partners and blindfolded them and led them down empty corridors at breakneck speeds, as an experiment in trust. We made collages about protecting the environment. We did skits about navigating the emotional crises of seventh and eighth grade. We sang along while advisors played songs by Cat Stevens. We wrote haikus on the theme of friendship and read them aloud:

A friend stands by you
Even when you're in trouble
So it's not so bad.

A friend is a person
You think you can depend on
And usually trust.

My own contribution to this exercise—

You get a haircut
Ordinary people laugh
Do friends? No, they don't.

—referred to certain realities at my junior high, not in the group. People in the group, even the people I didn't consider friends, weren't allowed to laugh at you that way. This was one reason I'd joined in the first place.

The group was called Fellowship—no definite article, no modifier—and it was sponsored by the First Congregational Church, with some help from the Evangelical United Church of Christ down the street. Most of the kids in seventh- and eighth-grade Fellowship had come up together through Sunday school at First Congregational and knew each other in almost cousinlike ways. We'd seen each other in miniature sport coats and clip-on ties or in plaid jumpers with velveteen bows, and we'd spent long minutes sitting in pews and staring at each other's defenseless parents while they worshipped, and one morning in the church basement, during a spirited singing of "Jesus Loves the Little Children," we'd all watched a little girl in white tights wet herself dramatically. Having been through these experiences together, we'd moved on into Fellowship with minimal social trauma.

The trouble began in ninth grade. Ninth-graders had their own separate Fellowship group, as if in recognition of the particular toxicity of ninth-grade adolescence, and the first few ninth-grade meetings, in September 1973, attracted rafts of newcomers who looked cooler and tougher and more experienced than most of us Congregational kids. There were girls with mouth-watering names like Julie Wolfrum and Brenda Pahmeier. There were guys with incipient beards and foot-long hair. There was a statuesque blond girl who incessantly practiced the guitar part to "The Needle and the Damage Done." All these kids raised their hands when our advisors asked who was planning to participate in the group's first weekend country retreat, in October.

I raised my hand, too. I was a Fellowship veteran and I liked retreats. But I was small and squeaky and a lot more articulate than I was mature, and from this stressful vantage the upcoming retreat looked less like a Fellowship event than like the kind of party I was ordinarily not invited to.

Luckily, my parents were out of the country. They were in the middle of their second trip to Europe, letting themselves be entertained by their Austrian business friends, at Austrian expense. I was spending the last three weeks of October as the ward of various neighbors, and it fell to one of them, Celeste Schwilck, to drive me down to First Congregational late on a Friday afternoon. In the passenger seat of the Schwilcks' burgundy Oldsmobile, I opened a letter that my mother had sent to me from London. The letter began with the word "Dearest," which my mother never seemed to realize was a more invasive and less endearing word than "Dear." Even if I'd been inclined to miss her, which I wasn't, the "Dearest" would have reminded me why I shouldn't. I put the letter, unread, into a paper bag with the dinner that Mrs. Schwilck had made me.

I was wearing my jeans and desert boots and windbreaker, my antianxiety ensemble. In the church parking lot, thirty-five kids in denim were throwing Frisbees and tuning guitars, smoking cigarettes, swapping desserts, and jockeying for rides in cars driven by the more glamorous young advisors. We were going to Shannondale, a camp in the Ozarks three hours south of St. Louis. For a ride this long, it was imperative to avoid the car of Social Death, which was typically filled with girls in shapeless slacks and boys whose sense of humor was substandard. I had nothing against these kids except a desperate fear of being taken for one of them. I dropped my bags on a pile of luggage and ran to secure a place in a safe car with a mustached seminarian and some smart, quiet Congregationalists who liked to play Ghost.

It was the season in Missouri when dusk crept up on you. Returning for my bags, I couldn't find my dinner. Car doors were slamming, engines starting. I ran around canvassing the people who hadn't left yet. Had anybody seen my paper bag? Five minutes into the retreat, I was already losing my cool. And this wasn't even the worst of it, because it was possible that, even now, in one of the glamorous cars, *somebody was reading my mother's letter*. I felt like an Air Force officer who'd let a nuclear warhead go missing.

I ran back to my chosen car and reported, with ornate self-disgust, that I'd lost my dinner. But the mustached seminarian almost welcomed my loss. He said that each person in the car could give me a small piece of dinner, and nobody would be hungry, and everybody would be fed. In the gathering dark, as we drove south out of the city, girls kept handing me food. I could feel their fingers as I took it.

On my only Boy Scout weekend, two years earlier, the leaders of the Bison Patrol had left us Tenderfeet to pitch our tents in steady rain. The leaders hung out with their friends in better-organized patrols who had brought along steaks and sodas and paraffin fire starters and great quantities of dry, seasoned firewood. When we young Bisons stopped by to warm ourselves, our leaders ordered us back to our sodden campsite. Late in the evening, the Scoutmaster consoled us with Silly Sally jokes that the older Scouts didn't want to listen to anymore. ("One time when Silly Sally was in the woods, an old man said to her, 'Silly Sally, I want you to take off all your clothes!' and Silly Sally said, 'Why, that's silly, because I'm sure they won't fit you!'") I came home from the weekend wet, hungry, tired, dirty, and furious. My father, hating all things military, was happy to excuse me from the Scouts, but he insisted that I participate in some activity, and my mother suggested Fellowship.

At Fellowship camps there were girls in halter tops and cut-offs. Each June, the seventh-and-eighth-grade group went down to Shannondale for five days and did maintenance for the church there, using scythes and paint rollers. The camp was near the Current River, a spring-fed, gravel-bottomed stream on which we took a float trip every year. My first summer, after the social discouragements of seventh grade, I wanted to toughen up my image and make myself more stupid, and I was trying to do this by continually exclaiming, "Son of a *bitch*!" Floating on the Current, I marveled at every green vista: "Son of a *bitch*!" This irritated my canoe mate, who, with each repetition, responded no less mechanically, "Yes, you certainly are one."

Our canoe was a thigh-fryer, an aluminum reflector oven. The day after the float trip, I was redder than the red-haired seventh-grader Bean but not quite as red as the most popular eighth-grade boy, Peppel, onto whose atrociously sunburned back Bean spilled an entire bowl of chicken-noodle soup that had just come off the boil. It was Bean's fate to make mistakes like this. He had a squawky voice and slide-rule sensibilities and an all-around rough time in Fellowship, where the prevailing ethic of honesty and personal growth licensed kids like Peppel to shout, "Jesus Christ! You're not just clumsy physically, you're clumsy with other people's feelings! You've got to learn how to watch out for other people!"

Bean, who was also in Boy Scouts, quit Fellowship soon after this, leaving me and my own clumsiness to become inviting targets for other people's honesty. In Shannondale the next summer, I was playing cards with the seventh-grader MacDonald, a feline-mannered girl whose granny glasses and Carole King frizz both attracted me and made me nervous, and in a moment of Beanish inspiration I decided it would be a funny joke to steal a look at MacDonald's cards while she was in the bathroom. But MacDonald failed to see the humor. Her skin was so clear that every emotion she experienced, no matter how mild, registered as some variety of blush. She began to call me "Cheater" even as I insisted, with a guilty smirk, that I hadn't seen her cards. She called me "Cheater" for the remainder of the trip. Leaving Shannondale, we all wrote farewell notes to each other, and MacDonald's note to me began *Dear Cheater* and concluded *I hope someday you'll learn there's more to life than cheating.*

Four months later, I certainly hadn't learned this lesson. The well-being I felt in returning to Shannondale as a ninth-grader, in wearing jeans and racing through the woods at night, was acquired mainly by fraud. I had to pretend to be a kid who naturally said "shit" a lot, a kid who hadn't written a book-length report on plant physiology, a kid who didn't enjoy calculating absolute stellar magnitudes on his new six-function Texas Instruments calculator, or else I might find myself exposed the way I'd been exposed not long ago in English class, where an athlete had accused me of preferring the dictionary to any other book, and my old friend Manley, whom I'd turned to for refutation of this devastating slander, had smiled at me and quietly confirmed, "He's right, Jon." Storming into the Shannondale boys' barn, identifying luggage from the Social Death car and claiming a bunk as far as I could get from it, I relied on the fact that my Fellowship friends went to different junior high schools and didn't know that I was Social Death myself.

Outside, I could hear tight cliques in desert boots crunching along on the Ozark flint gravel. Up by the Shannondale community center, in a cluster of Fellowship girls with wavy album-art hair and personalities that were sweet the way bruises on a peach are sweet, two unfamiliar tough guys in army jackets were calling and responding in high, femmy voices. One guy had lank hair and sufficient hormones for a downy Fu Manchu. He called out, "Dearest Jonathan!" The other guy, who was so fair he seemed not to have eyebrows or eyelashes, responded, "Oh, dearest Jonathan!"

"Heh heh heh. Dearest Jonathan."

"Dearest Jonathan!"

I turned on my heel and ran back into the woods, veered off into tree litter, and cowered in the dark. The retreat was now officially a disaster. It was some consolation, however, that people in Fellowship called me Jon, never Jonathan. As far as the tough guys knew, Dearest Jonathan might be anybody. Dearest Jonathan might still be up in Webster Groves, looking for his paper bag. If I could somehow avoid the two thieves all weekend, they might never figure out whose dinner they'd eaten.

The thieves made my task a little easier, as the group assembled in the community center, by sticking together and sitting down outside the Fellowship circle. I entered the room late, with my head low, and crowded into the antipodal portion of the circle, where I had friends.

"If you want to be part of this group," the youth minister, Bob Mutton, told the thieves, "join the circle."

Mutton was unafraid of tough guys. He wore an army jacket and talked like a pissed-off tough guy himself. You made yourself look childish, not cool, if you defied him. Mutton oversaw the entire Fellowship operation, with its 250 kids and several dozen advisors, and he looked rather scarily like Jesus—not the Renaissance Jesus, with the long Hellenic nose, but the more tormented Jesus of the northern Gothic. Mutton's eyes were blue and set close together below mournfully knitted eyebrows. He had coarse tangles of chestnut hair that hung over his collar and fell across his forehead in a canted mass; his goatee was a thick reddish bush into which he liked to insert Hauptmann's cigars. When he wasn't smoking or chewing on a Hauptmann's, he held a rolled-up magazine or a fireplace tool or a stick or a pointer and slapped his opposite palm with it. Talking to him, you could never be sure if he was going to laugh and nod and agree with you, or whether he was going to nail you with his favorite judgment: "That is . . . *such bullshit.*"

Since every word out of my mouth was arguably bullshit, I

was trying to steer clear of Mutton. Fellowship was a class I was never going to be the best student in; I was content to pull down B's and C's in honesty and openness. For the night's first exercise, in which each of us divulged how we hoped to grow on this retreat, I offered the bland goal of "developing new relationships." (My actual goal was to avoid certain new relationships.) Then the group split into a series of dyads and small groups for sensitivity training. The advisors tried to shuffle us, to break down cliques and force new interactions, but I was practiced at picking out and quickly nabbing partners who were neither Deathly nor good friends, and I brought my techniques to bear on the task of avoiding the thieves. I sat facing a schoolteacher's kid, a nice boy with an unfortunate penchant for talking about Gandalf, and closed my eyes and felt his face with my fingertips and let him feel mine. We formed five-person groups and interlocked our bodies to create machines. We regrouped as a plenum and lay down in a zigzagging circle, our heads on our neighbors' bellies, and laughed collectively.

I was relieved to see the thieves participating in these exercises. Once you let a stranger palpate your face, even if you did it with a smirk or a sneer, you became implicated in the group and were less likely to ridicule it on Monday. I had an inkling, too, that the exercises cost the thieves more than they cost me: that people who stole sack dinners were in a far unhappier place than I was. Although they were obviously my enemies, I envied them their long hair and their rebellious clothes, which I wasn't allowed to have, and I half admired the purity of their adolescent anger, which contrasted with my own muddle of self-consciousness and silliness and posturing. Part of why kids like this scared me was that they seemed authentic.

"Just a reminder," Mutton said before we dispersed for the night. "The three rules around here are no booze. No sex. And no drugs. Also, if you find out that *somebody else* has broken a rule, you have to come and tell me or tell one of the advisors. Otherwise it's the same as if you broke the rule yourself."

Mutton cast a glowering eye around the circle. The dinner thieves seemed greatly amused.

As an adult, when I say the words "Webster Groves" to people I've just met, I'm often informed that I grew up in a suffocatingly wealthy, insular, conformist town with a punitive social hierarchy. The twenty-odd people who have told me this over the years have collectively spent, by my estimate, about twenty minutes in Webster Groves, but each of them went to college in the seventies and eighties, and a fixture of sociology curricula in that era was a 1966 CBS documentary called *16 in Webster Groves*. The film, an early experiment in hour-long prime-time sociology, reported on the attitudes of suburban sixteen-year-olds. I've tried to explain that the Webster Groves depicted in it bears minimal resemblance to the friendly, unpretentious town I knew when I was growing up. But it's useless to contradict TV; people look at me with suspicion, or hostility, or pity, as if I'm deeply in denial.

According to the documentary's host, Charles Kuralt, Webster Groves High School was ruled by a tiny elite of "soshies" who made life gray and marginal for the great majority of students who weren't "football captains," "cheerleaders," or "dance queens." Interviews with these all-powerful soshies revealed a student body obsessed with grades, cars, and money. CBS repeatedly flashed images of the largest houses in Webster Groves; of the town's several thousand small and medium-sized houses there were no shots at all. For no apparent reason but the sheer visual grotesqueness of it, the filmmakers included nearly a minute of footage of grownups in tuxedos and cocktail dresses rock-and-roll dancing at a social club. In a disappointed tone, as if to suggest just how oppressive the town was, Kuralt reported that the number of tough kids and drinkers at the high school was "*very* low," and although he allowed that a "minority twenty percent" of sixteen-year-olds did place high value on intelligence, he was quick to inject a note of Orwellian portent: "That kind of thinking can imperil your social standing at Webster High."

The film wasn't entirely wrong about Webster High in the mid-sixties. My brother Tom, though not one of the film's 688 eponymous sixteen-year-olds (he was born a year late), remembers little about his high-school years besides accumulating good grades and drifting in social backwaters with all the other nonsoshies; his main recreation was bombing around with friends who had cars. Nor was the film wrong about the town's prevailing conservatism: Barry Goldwater had carried Webster Groves in 1964.

The problem with *16* was tonal. When Kuralt, with a desperate grin, asked a group of Webster Groves parents whether a civil rights march wouldn't maybe "sort of inject some life into things around here," the parents recoiled from him as if he were insane; and the filmmakers, unable to imagine that you could be a nice person and still not want your sixteen-year-old in a civil rights march, cast Webster Groves as a nightmare of mind control and soulless materialism. "Youth dreams, we had believed, of adventure," Kuralt voice-overed. "But three-quarters of these teenagers listed as their main goal in life a good-paying job, money, success. And we had thought that, at sixteen, you are filled with yearning and dissatisfaction. But ninety percent say they like it in Webster Groves. Nearly half said they wouldn't mind staying here *for the rest of their lives*." Kuralt laid ominous emphasis on this final fact. The most obvious explanation for it—that CBS had stumbled onto an unusually congenial community—seemed not to have crossed his mind.

The film's broadcast, on February 25, 1966, drew so many angry phone calls and letters from Webster Groves that the network put together an extraordinary hour-long follow-up, *Webster Groves Revisited*, and aired it two months later. Here Kuralt came as close to apologizing as he could without using the word "sorry." He offered conciliatory footage of soshies watching the February broadcast and clutching their heads at the pompous things they'd said on camera; he conceded that children who grew up in safe environments might still become adventurers as adults.

The core value in Webster Groves, the value whose absence in *16* most enraged its citizens, was a kind of apolitical niceness. The membership of First Congregational may have been largely Republican, but it consistently chose liberal pastors. The church's minister in the 1920s had informed the congregation that his job was "clinical," not personal. ("The successful minister is a psychoanalyst," he said. "If that thought shocks you, let me tell you that Jesus was the master psychoanalyst of all time. Can a minister do better than follow Him?") In the 1930s, the lead pastor was a fervid socialist who wore a beret and smoked cigarettes while riding to and from the church on a bicycle. He was succeeded by an Army combat veteran, Ervine Inglis, who preached pacifism throughout the Second World War.

Bob Roessel, the son of a local Republican lawyer, grew up going to the church under its socialist pastor and spent his summers with an uncle in New Mexico who administered the Federal Writers' Project in the state for the Works Projects Administration. Traveling around the Southwest, Roessel fell in love with Navajo culture and decided to become a missionary—an ambition that survived until he went to seminary and met actual working missionaries, who spoke of leading savages from darkness into light. Roessel went and asked Ervine Inglis, whose proclivities were Unitarian (he didn't believe in the effectiveness of prayer, for example), if a person could be both Christian *and* Navajo. Inglis said yes. Abandoning the seminary, Roessel married the daughter of a Navajo medicine man and dedicated his life to serving his adoptive people. On visits to Webster Groves to see his mother, he set up a table at First Congregational and sold blankets and silver jewelry to raise money for the tribe. He gave barn-burning speeches on the greatness of the Navajos, telling church members that their Midwestern world, their shady lawns and good schools and middle-management jobs at Monsanto, would be *heaven* to his other people. "The Navajos," he said, "have nothing. They live in the desert with nothing. And yet the Navajos have something you don't have: the Navajos believe in God."

In the fall of 1967, the church's new associate minister, Duane Estes, gathered together sixteen teenagers and one seminary student and made a proposition: How would they like to form a group to raise money to go to Arizona over spring vacation to help the Navajos? Out in the town of Rough Rock, Bob Roessel was starting a "demonstration school," the first Indian school in the country for which the Bureau of Indian Affairs would be ceding control to a local Indian school board, and he needed volunteers to work in the community. First Congregational's old senior-high group, Pilgrim Fellowship, had lately fallen on hard times (this may have had something to do with the black Pilgrim hats its members were expected to wear at meetings). Estes, a former prep-school chaplain and football coach, jettisoned the word "Pilgrim" (also the hats) and proposed a different kind of pilgrimage, a football coach's pilgrimage: Let's go out in the world and hit somebody! He'd anticipated that a couple of station wagons would suffice for the Arizona trip, but by the time the group left for Rough Rock, a day after the shooting of Martin Luther King, Jr., it filled a chartered bus.

The lone seminary student, Bob Mutton, was there on the

bus with all the clean-cut suburban kids, sporting big sideburns and wearing his outsider's glower. Mutton had grown up in a blue-collar town outside Buffalo. He'd been a bad boy in high school, a pursuer of girls in the hulking '49 Buick convertible that he and his father, a machinist, had fixed up. It happened that one girl whom Mutton was particularly chasing belonged to a local church group, and the group's leader took an interest in him, urging him to apply to college. He ended up at Elmhurst College, a church-affiliated school outside Chicago. For a couple of years, he kept up his antisocial pursuits; he hung out with bad boys and he liked them. Then, in his fourth year of immersion in Elmhurst, he announced to his parents that he was going to marry a classmate, a working-class Chicago girl, and go to seminary. His father didn't like the seminary idea—couldn't a person be a Christian and still go to law school?—but Mutton felt he had a calling, and he enrolled at Eden Theological Seminary, in Webster Groves, in the fall of 1966.

It was a time when schools like Eden were attracting students who coveted the military draft classification, IV-D, which was given to seminarians. Mutton and his first-year friends had rowdy parties in the dorm and laughed in the faces of the pious upperclassmen who complained about the noise. The longer Mutton and his wife stayed in Webster Groves, though, the less social life they had. Webster Groves wasn't a town of blue bloods, but it was full of upward middle-class striving, and the Muttons seldom met young couples they felt comfortable with. Mutton ate with his fork in his fist, like a shovel. He drove a car that burned almost as much oil as gas. He paid his school bills by working as a tile layer. When the time came to choose his fieldwork, in his second year at Eden, he was one of only two people in his class to sign up for youth ministry. He'd become aware of a huge submerged population of lost teenagers, some of them good students, some of them roughnecks, some of them just misfits, all of them undernourished by the values of their parents, and, unlike CBS, he gave them full credit for yearning and dissatisfaction. He'd been a kid like this himself. Still was one, basically.

In churches the size of First Congregational, senior-high groups typically have thirty or forty members—the number that Fellowship had attracted in its first year. By June 1970, when First Congregational hired Mutton to replace Duane Estes, the group's membership had doubled to eighty, and in the first two years of Mutton's ministry, at the historical apex of American disenchantment with institutional authority, it doubled again. Every weekday after school, church elders had to pick their way through teenage feet in sandals, Keds, and work boots. There was a clutch of adoring girls who practically lived in Mutton's office, vying for space on his beat-up sofa, beneath his psychedelic Jesus poster. Between this office and the church's meeting hall, dozens of other kids in embroidered smocks and denim shirts were playing guitars in competing keys while cigarette smoke whitely filled the long-necked soda bottles into which everyone persisted in dropping butts despite complaints from the vending-machine company.

"I'll ask the youth minister to ask them again not to do that," the infinitely patient church secretary kept promising the company.

Kids from other churches joined the group for the romance of Arizona, for the twenty-hour marathons of live music that the bus rides in both directions quickly became, and for the good-looking crowds that came to the acoustic and electric concerts that Fellowship musicians held in the church on Friday nights. The biggest draw, though, was Mutton himself. As the overplayed song then had it, "To sing the blues / You've got to live the dues," and Mutton's blue-collar background and his violent allergy to piousness made him a beacon of authenticity to the well-groomed kids of Webster Groves. Working with adolescents was notoriously time-consuming, but Mutton, lacking a social life, had time for it. In his simmering and strutting and cursing, he stood for the adolescent alienation that nobody else over twenty in Webster Groves seemed to understand.

Mutton on a basketball court was a maniac with blazing eyes and a soaking-wet T-shirt. He whipped the ball to weak players at the same finger-breaking velocity as he did to strong ones; if you didn't get your feet planted when he was taking the ball to the basket, he knocked you down and ran right over you. If you were a Navajo elder and you saw a busload of middle-class white kids arriving on your land with guitars and paintbrushes, and if you went to Mutton and asked him why the group had come, he gave you the only right answer: "We came here mostly for ourselves." If you were a Fellowship member and you happened to be riding in his car when he stopped to buy Communion supplies, he turned to you like a peer and asked for your help: "What kind of wine should I be looking for?" He talked about sex the same way. He wondered what you thought of the European idea that Americans were passive in bed, and whether you knew the joke about the Frenchman who found a woman lying on a beach and started having sex with her, and his friends pointed out that she was dead ("Oh, sorry, I thought she was American"). He seemed ready to be guided by your judgment when he asked you what you made of certain New Testament miracles, like the loaves and the fishes. What did you think really happened there? And maybe you ventured the guess that some of the five thousand people who came to hear Jesus had had provisions hidden in their robes, and Jesus' message of brotherhood moved them to share their privately hoarded food, and giving begat giving, and this was how the five thousand were fed. "So a kind of miracle of socialism?" Mutton said. "That would be miracle enough for me."

"Parents complaining because their high-school youngster spends too much time at church!" the *St. Louis Globe-Democrat* exclaimed in a full-page article about Fellowship in November 1972. "Parents forbidding a high schooler to go to church as a punishment!" Some parents, both inside and outside First Congregational, thought that Fellowship might even be a cult. Mutton in poor light was mistakable for Charles Manson, and it was unsettling how much the kids looked forward to Sunday nights, saving their favorite, most worn-out clothes for the occasion and throwing fits if they missed even one meeting. But most parents recognized that, given the state of intergenerational relations in the early seventies, things could have been a whole lot worse. Mutton had the trust of the church's senior minister, Paul Davis, and key support from several leading church elders who had gone on early Arizona trips and come home sold on Fellowship. A few conservative congregants complained to Davis about Mutton's style, his cigars and his obscenities, and Davis listened to the complaints with active sympathy, nodding and amiably wincing and repeating, in his extraordinarily soothing voice, that he understood their concerns and was really grateful that they had gone to the trouble of sharing them with him. Then he closed his office door and took no action of any kind.

Mutton was like a bass lure cast into a pond that hadn't been fished in thirty years. No sooner had he taken over Fellowship than he was mobbed by troubled kids who couldn't tolerate their parents but still needed an adult in their lives. Kids came and told him, as they'd never told anyone else, that their fathers got drunk and hit them. They brought him dreams for his interpretation. They queued up outside his office door, waiting for individual conferences, suffering for not being the lucky person alone with him behind his closed door, and feeling that not even the joy of finally getting into the office could compensate for the pain of waiting. Everybody and his brother were doing drugs. Kids were watering the family Gilbey's and dropping acid in school bathrooms, smoking specially adulterated banana peels, popping parental antihistamines and grandparental nitroglycerin, consuming nutmeg in vomitous quantities, filling empty milk cartons with beer and drinking in public, exhaling pot smoke into stove hoods or the absorbant insulation of basement ceilings, and then heading on down to church. Three boys from good families were caught toking in the First Congregational sanctuary itself. Mutton sat for hours trying to follow the words of a founding member of Fellowship lately released from the mental hospital where a lysergic brain-scrambling had landed him. When a Fellowship girl informed Mutton that she'd got drunk at a party and had had sex with three Fellowship boys in rapid succession, Mutton brought all four kids together in his office and, asserting a kind of patriarchal prerogative, made each boy apologize. A different girl, whose parents had confronted her with contraceptives that they'd found in her bedroom, refused to speak to them unless Mutton was summoned as a mediator. He was part Godfather and part Sorcerer's Apprentice, implicated in the lives of more and more families.

In September 1973, the month before the ninth-grade retreat at Shannondale, a gifted seventeen-year-old boy named MacDonald came to Mutton's office and told him there were no more challenges in his life. MacDonald was the older brother of the girl who'd been so disappointed in my cheating at cards. He was about to start college, and Mutton didn't follow up on the conversation; and a few weeks later MacDonald hanged himself. Mutton was devastated. He felt, at twenty-nine, overwhelmed and underprepared. He decided that he needed training as a therapist, and a parishioner at First Congregational kindly lent him five thousand dollars so that he could study with a prominent local Christian shrink.

. . .

It was years—decades—before I found out about any of this. I was a latecomer to Fellowship in the same way I was a latecomer to my own family. When need-to-know lists were being made up, I was always left off them. It was as if I went through life wearing a sign that said KEEP HIM IN THE DARK.

When my friend Weidman and I were discussing what a girl did when she masturbated, I thought I was holding up my side of the conversation rather well, but I must have said something wrong, because Weidman asked me, in the tone of a friendly professor, "You know what masturbation is, don't you?" I replied that, yes, of course, it was the bleeding, and the period, and so forth. In speech class, I failed to foresee the social penalties that a person might pay for bringing in his stuffed Kanga and Roo toys to illustrate his speech about Australian wildlife. Regarding drugs, I couldn't help noticing that a lot of kids at school were getting high to fortify themselves for classes. Missouri school-yard pot in 1973 was a weak, seedy product, and users had to take so many hits that they came inside reeking of smoke, the way the physical-science room reeked once a year, after the Distillation of Wood. But I was not a worldly fourteen-year-old. I didn't even know what to call the stuff that kids were smoking. The word "pot" to me had the quotation-marked ring of moms and teachers trying to sound hipper than they really were, which was unpleasantly close to a description of myself. I was determined to say "dope" instead, because that was what my friend Manley said, but this word, too, had a way of losing its cool on my tongue; I wasn't one hundred percent sure that actual pot-smokers called marijuana "dope," and the long "o" shriveled in my mouth like a raisin, and the word came out sounding more like "duip."

So if it had been me who crossed the Shannondale parking

lot on Saturday night and smelled burning hemp, I would have kept my mouth shut. The weekend was proving less disastrous than I'd feared. The two dinner thieves had made themselves scarce to the point of actually skipping mandatory activities, and I'd grown so bold as to involve my old Sunday-school friends in a game of Four Square, using a basketball. (At school, the year before, Manley and I had instigated a semi-ironic revival of Four Square at lunch hour, reconceiving it as a game of speed and English, and though Manley was too good an athlete to be sneered at, my own blithe advocacy of a grade-school girls' game was probably one reason my lab partner Lunte had been asked if I was a contemptible faggot and beaten up when he said no.) I'd sat in Ozark sunshine with my pretty, poetic friend Hoener and talked about Gregor Mendel and e. e. cummings. Late in the evening, I'd played Spades with an advisor I had a crush on, a high-school girl named Kortenhof, while somebody else crossed the parking lot and smelled the smoke.

The next morning, when we convened in the community center for what should have been a short, music-driven, Jesus-free Sunday service, the advisors all showed up together in a grim-faced phalanx. Mutton, who turned pale when he was angry, was practically blue-lipped.

"Last night," he said in a chalky voice, "some people broke the rules. Some people used drugs. And they know who they are, and they've got things to say to us. If you were one of those people, or if you knew about it and you didn't say anything, I want you to stand up now and tell us what happened."

Mutton took a step back, like a theatrical presenter, and six offenders rose. There were two girls, Hellman and Yanczer, with swollen, tear-stained faces; a peripheral Fellowship boy named Magner; the two thieves, the fair-haired one and the tough guy with the Fu Manchu; and a snide girl in tight clothes who seemed attached to them. The thieves looked at once miserable and defiant. They said they mumble mumble mumble.

"What? I didn't hear you," Mutton said.

"I said I got high in the parking lot and broke the rules," spat Fu Manchu.

A physical gap had opened between the rest of us and the delinquents, who stood ranged against one wall of the community center, some glaring, others crying, their thumbs all hooked on the pockets of their jeans. I felt like a little child who'd spent the weekend doing silly feckless things (Four Square!) while serious grownup shit was going down elsewhere.

The girl Hellman was the most upset. Even under normal circumstances, her eyes glistened and protruded a little, as if with the pressure of pent-up emotion, and now her whole face was glistening. "I'm so sorry!" she wailed to Mutton. Pressurized tears came spurting from her eyes, and she turned to face the rest of us. "I'm so sorry!"

Yanczer was a small, round-faced girl who tended to talk over her shoulder, leaning away from you, as if you'd temporarily changed her mind about leaving. She had her shoulder to the wall now. "I'm sorry, too," she said, looking at us sideways. "Although, at the same time I feel, like, what's the big deal?"

"We're a community here, that's the big deal," Mutton said. "We're allowed to do neat stuff because parents trust us. When people break the rules and undermine that trust, it hurts everyone in the community. It's possible that this could be the end of the group. This weekend."

The thieves were passing a smile back and forth.

"What are you two smiling at?" Mutton barked. "You think this is funny?"

"No," the fair one said, tossing his nearly white locks. "But this does seem a little extreme."

"Nobody's making you stay in this room. You can walk out the door any time you want. In fact, why don't you just leave. Both of you. You've been smirking the whole weekend. I'm sick of it."

The thieves exchanged corroborating looks and headed for the door, followed by the snide girl. This left Hellman, Yanczer, and Magner. The question was whether to banish them, too.

"If this is the way you treat the group," Mutton said, "if this is the kind of trust level here, why should we want to see you next week? We need to hear why you think you should still be allowed to be part of this group."

Hellman looked around at us, wide-eyed, beseeching. She said we couldn't banish her. She loved Fellowship! We'd practically saved her life! She cared about the group more than *anything*.

A pixie in faded coveralls countered, "If you care about the group, then why'd you bring these freakheads into it and get us all in trouble?"

"I wanted them to know what Fellowship was like," Hellman said, wringing her hands. "I thought we'd be good for them! I'm sorry!"

"Look, you can't control what your friends do," Mutton said. "You're only responsible for you."

"But I fucked up, too!" Hellman wailed.

"Right, and you're taking responsibility for it."

"But she fucked up!" the pixie in coveralls pointed out. "How is she 'taking responsibility' for it?"

"By standing up here and facing you guys," Mutton answered. "That is a very hard thing to do. That takes guts. No matter what you all decide to do, I want you to think about the guts these guys are showing, just by staying in this room with us."

There ensued an hour-long excruciation in which, one by

one, we addressed the three miscreants and told them how we felt. Girls rubbed ashes into denim and fidgeted with their Winston hard packs. Kids broke out in sobs at the thought of the group's being disbanded. Outside, crunching around on gravel, were the parents who'd driven down to give us rides home, but it was Fellowship procedure to confront crises without delay, and so we kept sitting there. Hellman and Yanczer and Magner alternately apologized and lashed out at us: What about forgiveness? Hadn't we ever broken rules ourselves?

I found the whole scene confusing. Hellman's confession had stamped her, in my mind, as a scary outcast stoner, the kind of marginal person I was afraid of and disdained at school, and yet she was acting as if she'd die if she couldn't come to Fellowship. I liked the group, too, or at least I had until this morning; but I certainly couldn't see myself dying without it. Hellman seemed to be having a more central and authentic Fellowship experience than the rules-abiding members she'd betrayed. Here was Mutton talking about how brave she was! When my turn came to speak, I said I was afraid my parents wouldn't let me go to Fellowship anymore, because they were so anti-drug, but I didn't think that anybody should be suspended.

It was past noon when we emerged from the community center, blinking in the strong light. The banished thieves were down by the picnic tables, tossing a Nerf football and laughing. We had decided to give Hellman and Yanczer and Magner a second chance, but the really important thing, Mutton said, was to go straight home and tell our parents what had happened. Each one of us had to take full responsibility for the group.

This was probably hardest for Hellman, who loved Fellowship in proportion to her father's unkindness to her at home, and for Yanczer. When Yanczer's mother was given the news, she threatened to call the police unless Yanczer went to her junior-high principal and narked out the friend who supplied her with drugs; this friend was Magner. It was a week of gruesome scenes, and yet somehow all three kids dragged themselves to Fellowship the following Sunday.

Only I still had a problem. The problem was my parents. Of the many things I was afraid of in those days—spiders, insomnia, fish hooks, school dances, hardball, heights, bees, urinals, puberty, music teachers, dogs, the school cafeteria, censure, older teenagers, jellyfish, locker rooms, boomerangs, popular girls, the high dive—I was probably most afraid of my parents. My father had almost never spanked me, but his anger had been Jehovan when he did. My mother possessed claws with which, when I was three or four years old and neighbor kids had filled my hair with Vaseline to achieve a kind of Baby Greaser effect, she'd repeatedly attacked my scalp between dousings of scalding-hot water. Her opinions were even sharper than her claws. You just didn't want to mess with her. I never would have dared, for example, to take advantage of her absence from the country and break her rules and wear jeans to school, because what if she found out?

Had I been able to talk to my parents right away, the retreat's momentum might have carried me. But they were still in Europe, and I daily became more convinced that they would forbid me to go to Fellowship—not only this, but they would yell at me, and not only this, but they would force me to hate the group—until I landed in a state of full-bore dread, as if *I* were the one who'd broken the rules. Before long, I was more afraid of confessing to the group's collective crime than I'd ever been of anything.

In Paris, my mother had her hair done at Elizabeth Arden and chatted with the widow of Pie Traynor, the Hall of Fame third baseman. In Madrid, she ate suckling pig at Casa Botín among crowds of Americans whose ugliness depressed her, but then she ran into the married couple who owned the hardware store in Webster Groves and who were also on vacation, and she felt better. The twenty-eighth of October she spent with my father in a first-class train compartment, traveling to Lisbon, and noted in her travel diary: *Nice 29th anniversary—being together all day.* In Lisbon, she received an airmail letter in which I didn't say a word about the Fellowship retreat.

My brother Bob and I were waiting at the airport in St. Louis on Halloween. Coming off the plane, my parents looked amazingly fit and cosmopolitan and lovable. I found myself smiling uncontrollably. This was supposed to have been the evening for my confession, but it seemed potentially awkward to involve Bob in it, and not until he'd returned to his apartment in the city did I understand how much harder it would be to face my parents without him. Since Bob usually came to dinner on Sunday nights, and since Sunday was only four days away, I decided to delay my disclosure until he came back. Hadn't I already delayed two weeks?

On Sunday morning, my mother mentioned that Bob had other plans and wasn't coming to dinner.

I considered never saying anything at all. But I didn't see how I could go back and face the group. The anguish in Shannondale had had the mysterious effect of making me feel more intimately committed to Fellowship, rather than less, as if we were all now bound together by shame, the way strangers who'd slept together might wake up feeling compassion for each other's embarrassment and fall in love on that basis. To my surprise, I found that I, too, like Hellman, loved the group.

At dinner that afternoon, I sat between my parents and didn't eat.

"Do you not feel well?" my mother finally said.

"I'm supposed to tell you about something that happened at Fellowship," I said, keeping my eyes on my plate. "On the retreat. Six kids on the retreat—smuiked some duip."

"Did what?"

"'Duip'? What?"

"Smuiked marijuana," I said.

My mother frowned. "Who was it? Any of your friends?"

"No, mostly new kids."

"Oh, uh-huh."

And this was the extent of their response: inattention and approval. I felt too elated to stop and wonder why. It was possible that bad stuff had happened with my brothers and drugs in the sixties, stuff beside which my own secondhand offenses might have seemed ridiculously unworrisome to my parents. But nobody had told me anything. After dinner, buoyant with relief, I floated into Fellowship and learned that I'd been given the lead in the three-act farce *Mumbo-Jumbo* that was going to be the group's big winter moneymaker. Hellman was playing a demure young woman who turns out to be a strangler; Magner was playing the evil swami Omahandra; and I was the callow, bossy, anxious college student Dick.

The man who trained Mutton as a therapist, George Benson, was Fellowship's hidden theoretician. In his book *Then Joy Breaks Through* (Seabury Press, 1972), Benson ridiculed the notion that spiritual rebirth was "simply a beautiful miracle for righteous people." He insisted that "personal growth" was the "only frame of reference from which Christian faith makes sense in our modern world." To survive in an age of anxiety and skepticism, Christianity had to reclaim the radicalism of Jesus' ministry, and the central message of the Gospels, in Benson's reading of them, was the importance of honesty and confrontation and struggle. Jesus' relationship with Peter in particular looked a lot like the psychoanalytic relationship:

> Insight is not good enough. The assurances of others are not good enough. Acceptance within a continuing relationship which denies reassurance (it's usually false anyway) and thereby brings the sufferer to an awareness of his need to evaluate and accept himself—this brings change.

Benson recounted his treatment of a young woman with severe symptoms of hippiedom—drug abuse, promiscuity, sensationally bad personal hygiene (at one point, roaches come swarming out of her purse)—and he compared her progress to that of Peter, who initially resisted Jesus, then monstrously idealized him, then fell into despair at the prospect of termination, and was finally saved by internalizing the relationship.

Mutton had first gone to Benson soon after he became an associate minister. He suddenly had so much influence over the teenagers in his charge that he was afraid he might start acting out, and Benson had told him he was right to be afraid. He made Mutton name aloud the things he was tempted to do, so as to make himself less likely to do them. It was a kind of psychic homeopathy, and Mutton brought the method back to his Fellowship leadership supervisions, where, every week, behind closed doors, in the church parlor, he and the advisors took turns making each other uncomfortable, inoculating themselves against temptations to misuse their power, airing their personal issues so as not to inflict them on the kids. Photocopies of *Then Joy Breaks Through* began to circulate among Fellowship advisors. The Authentic Relationship, as exemplified by Jesus and Peter, became the group's Grail—its alternative to the passive complicity of drug-using communities, its rebuke to traditional pastoral notions of "comforting" and "enabling."

As soon as Mutton entered training with Benson, following MacDonald's suicide, the spirit of Fellowship began to change. Part of the change was cultural, the waning of a hippie moment; part of it was Mutton's own growing up, his diminishing need for seventeen-year-old buddies, his increasing involvement with his outside clients. But after the Shannondale debacle there were no more wholesale rule violations, and Fellowship became less of a one-man show, less of an improvised happening, more of a well-oiled machine. By the time I started tenth grade, the senior-high group was paying small monthly salaries to half a dozen young advisors. Their presence made it all the easier for me to steer clear of Mutton, whose habit of calling me "Franzone!" (it rhymed with "trombone") somehow confirmed that he and I had no real relationship. It no sooner would have occurred to me to go to him with my troubles than to confide in my parents.

The advisors, on the other hand, were like older brothers and sisters. My favorite was Bill Symes, who'd been a founding member of Fellowship in 1967. He was in his early twenties now and studying religion at Webster University. He had shoulders like a two-oxen yoke, a ponytail as thick as a pony's tail, and feet requiring the largest size of Earth Shoes. He was a good musician, a passionate attacker of steel acoustical guitar strings. He liked to walk into Burger King and loudly order two Whoppers with no meat. If he was losing a Spades game, he would take a card out of his hand, tell the other players, "Play this suit!" and then lick the card and stick it to his forehead facing out. In discussions, he liked to lean into other people's space and bark at them. He said, "You better deal with that!" He said, "Sounds to me like *you've* got a problem that *you're* not talking about!" He said, "You know what? I don't think you believe *one word* of what you just said to me!" He said, "Any resistance will be met with an *aggressive* response!" If you hesitated when he moved to hug you, he backed away and spread his arms wide and goggled at you with raised eyebrows, as if to say, "Hello? Are you going to hug me, or what?" If he wasn't playing guitar he was reading Jung, and if he wasn't reading Jung he was bird-watching, and if he wasn't birdwatching he was practicing tai chi, and if you came up to him during his practice and asked him how he would defend himself if you tried to mug him with a gun, he would demonstrate, in dreamy Eastern motion, how to remove a wallet from a back pocket and hand it over. Listening to the radio in his VW Bug, he might suddenly cry out, "I want to hear . . . 'La Grange' by ZZ Top!" and slap the dashboard. The radio would then play "La Grange."

One weekend in 1975, Mutton and Symes and the other advisors attended a pastoral retreat sponsored by the United Church of Christ. The Fellowship gang rode in like Apaches of confrontation, intending to shock and educate the old-fashioned hand-holders and enablers. They performed a mock supervision, sitting in a tight circle while seventy or eighty ministers sat around them and observed. Inside this fishbowl, Mutton turned to Symes and asked him, "When are you going to cut your hair?"

Symes had known in advance that he was going to be the "volunteer." But his ponytail was very important to him, and the subject was explosive.

Mutton asked him again, "When are you going to cut your hair?"

"Why should I cut my hair?"

"When are you going to grow up and be a leader?"

While the other advisors kept their heads low and the enabling and comforting older clergy looked on, Mutton began to beat up on Symes. "You're committed to social justice and personal growth," he said. "Those are your values."

Symes made a stupid-face. "Duh! Your values, too."

"Well, and who are the people who most need to hear your

voice? People who look like you, or people who don't look like you?"

"Both. Everyone."

"But what if your attachment to your *style* is becoming a barrier to doing what's most important to you? What's the problem with cutting your hair?"

"I don't want to cut my hair!" Symes said, his voice breaking.

"That is *such bullshit*," Mutton said. "Where do you want to fight your battles? Do you want to be fighting about your tie-dye T-shirt and your painter's pants? Or do you want to be fighting over civil rights? Immigrant workers' rights? Women's rights? Compassion for the disenfranchised? If these are the battles that matter to you, when are you going to grow up and cut your hair?"

"I don't know—"

"When are you going to grow up and accept your authority?"

"I don't know! Bob. I don't know!"

Mutton could have been asking himself the same questions. Fellowship had been meeting in a Christian church for nearly a decade, whole years had gone by in which no Bible had been seen, "Jesus Christ" was the thing you said when somebody spilled soup on your sunburn, and George Benson, in his supervision of Mutton, wanted to know what the story was. Was this a Christian group or not? Was Mutton willing to stick his neck out and own up to his belief in God and Christ? Was he willing to claim his ministry? Mutton was getting similar questions from some of the advisors. They wanted to know on whose authority honesty and confrontation had become the central values of the group. On Mutton's authority? Why Mutton's? Who he? If the group wanted to be about more than Mutton and the group's adoration of him, then where did the authority reside?

To Mutton the answer was clear. If you took away Christ's divinity, you were left with "Kum Ba Ya." You were left with

"Let's hold hands and be nice to each other." Jesus' authority as a teacher—and whatever authority Mutton and company had as followers of his teachings—rested on His having had the balls to say, "I am the fulfillment of the prophecies, I am the Jews' gift to mankind, I am the son of Man," and to let Himself be nailed to a cross to back it up. If you couldn't take that step in your own mind, if you couldn't refer to the Bible and celebrate Communion, how could you call yourself a Christian?

The question, which Mutton raised in supervision, pissed off Symes extravagantly. The group already had its own rituals and liturgies and holy days, its candles, its Joni Mitchell songs, its retreats and spring trips. Symes was amazed that Mutton, with his training in Freud and Jung, wasn't repelled by the childishness and regression of Christian ceremony. "'How can we call ourselves Christians?'" he echoed, goggling at Mutton. "Uh, how about by . . . *trying to live like Christ and follow his teachings?* What do we need to eat somebody's blood and body for? That is so unbelievably primitive. When *I* want to feel close to God, I don't read Corinthians. I go out and work with poor people. I put myself in loving relationships. Including my relationship with *you*, Bob."

This was the classic position of liberal religion, and Symes could afford to take it because he didn't need to humble himself, because he didn't have to be the Jesus of Fellowship. Mutton was the bearded young machinist's son who preached radical stuff to the young and the marginalized, hung out with characters of dubious morality, attracted a cadre of devoted disciples, wrestled with the temptations of ego, and had become, by local standards, wildly popular. Now he was nearing his thirty-second birthday. He would be leaving soon, and he wanted to complete the shift in the group's focus away from himself and toward religion.

With Symes acting less like a tractable Peter than an ob-

streperous Jung, it fell to another seminarian, a red-haired former bad boy named Chip Jahn, to stand up at the end of a
Sunday-night meeting in 1975 and make a confession. Jahn had
been nineteen when Mutton put him in charge of a work camp
in Missouri's southeastern Bootheel. He'd spent a month with
kids just two and three years younger than he was, making do
with a food budget that was cut in half at the last minute, begging bushels of field corn from local farmers, trying to cook it
into casseroles seasoned with strips of bologna from pirated
government-issue school lunches. Since then, he'd decided to
enter the ministry, but he still had the manner of a pugnacious
sailor, leaning against walls with his arms crossed and his sleeves
rolled up tightly over his biceps; usually, when he addressed the
group, he had trouble keeping his face straight, as if it never
ceased to amuse him that he was working in a church. But now,
when he stood up to make his confession, he looked weirdly
serious.

"I want to talk about something that's important to me," he
said. He was holding up a book that flopped over like a raw
steak. When the group realized that the book was a Bible, an
uneasy silence settled on the room. I wouldn't have been a lot
more surprised if he'd been holding up a copy of *Penthouse*.
"This is important to me," Jahn said.

My dream as a tenth-grader was to be elected to the Advisory
Council, which was the in-crowd of sixteen kids who adjudicated
rule violations and helped the advisors run senior-high Fellowship. Twice a year, in what were unabashedly popularity con-
tests, the group elected eight kids to one-year council terms,
and it seemed to me that I had some chance of winning in the
spring. Somewhat mysteriously—it might simply have been

that my face was becoming familiar around church—I no longer felt like potential Social Death. I tried out for the group's fall play, *Any Number Can Die*, and was one of only two sophomores to get a part. On Sunday nights, when the big group broke into dyads for certain exercises, Advisory Council members came bounding across the room to partner up with me. They said, "Franzen! I want to get to know you better, because you seem like a really interesting person!" They said, "Franzen, I'm so happy you're in this group!" They said, "Franzen! I've been wanting to be your partner in something for weeks, but man, you're just too popular!"

It went to my head to feel noticed like this. On the year's last retreat, I nominated myself for Advisory Council. The full group gathered on Saturday night, after the ballots had been secretly tabulated, and we sat around a single candle. One by one, current members of the Advisory Council took new candles, lit them on the central candle, and moved into the crowd to present them to newly elected members. It was like watching fireworks; the crowd said "Ohhh!" as each winner was revealed. I pasted a smile on my face and pretended to be happy for the winners. But as candles approached me and passed me by and descended—"Ohhh!"—on other lucky souls, it was painfully clear how much more popular and mature than I the winners were. The ones getting the candles were the people who lounged around in semi-reclining, toboggan-style embraces or lay supine and propped their stockinged feet on nearby backs and shoulders, and who spoke as if they were doing genuine work on their relationships. The people who, if a newcomer was looking lost on a Sunday night, would race each other to be the first to introduce themselves. The people who knew how to look a friend in the eye and say, "I love you," the people who could break down and cry in front of the entire group, the people whom Mutton came up to from behind and put his arms around and nuzzled like a father lion, the people whom Mutton would have to have been Christlike not to favor. It might have struck me as odd that a group offering refuge from the cliquishness of high school, a group devoted to service to the marginalized, made such a huge deal of a ceremony in which precisely the smartest and most confident kids were anointed as leaders; but there were still two candles unaccounted for, and one of them was coming my way now, and this candle, instead of passing me by, was placed in my hands, and as I walked to the front of the room to join the new council in facing out to smile at the Fellowship that had elected us, all I could think of was how happy I was.

CENTRALLY LOCATED

KORTENHOF HAD HEARD of a high school where pranksters had put an automobile tire over the top of a thirty-foot flagpole, like a ring on a finger, and this seemed to him an impressive and elegant and beautiful feat that we at our high school ought to try to duplicate. Kortenhof was the son of a lawyer, and he had a lawyerly directness and a perpetual crocodile smile that made him fun company, if a little scary. Every day at lunch hour he led us outside to gaze at the flagpole and to hear his latest thoughts about accessorizing it with steel-belted radial tires. (Steel-belted radials, he said, would be harder for administrators to remove.) Eventually we all agreed that this was an exciting technical challenge worthy of a heavy investment of our time and energy.

The flagpole, which was forty feet tall, stood on an apron of concrete near the high school's main entrance, on Selma Avenue. It was too thick at the base to be shinnied up easily, and a fall from the top could be fatal. None of us had access to an extension ladder longer than twenty feet. We talked about building some sort of catapult, how spectacular a catapult would be, but airborne car tires were sure to do serious damage if they missed their mark, and cops patrolled Selma too frequently for us to risk getting caught with heavy equipment, assuming we could even build it.

The school itself could be a ladder, though. The roof was only six feet lower than the ball at the flagpole's crown, and we knew how to get to the roof. My friend Davis and I volunteered to build a Device, consisting of ropes and a pulley and a long board, that would convey a tire from the roof to the pole and drop it over. If the Device didn't work, we could try lassoing the pole with a rope, standing on a stepladder for added elevation, and sliding a tire down the rope. If this failed as well, it still might be possible, with a lot of luck, to gang-Frisbee a tire up and out and over.

Six of us—Kortenhof, Davis, Manley, Schroer, Peppel, and me—met up near the high school on a Friday night in March. Davis came with a stepladder on top of his parents' Pinto station wagon. There had been some trouble at home when his father saw the ladder, but Davis, who was smarter and less kind-hearted than his parent, had explained that the ladder belonged to Manley.

"Yes, but what are you doing with it?"

"Dad, it's Ben's ladder."

"I know, but what are you doing with it?"

"I just said! It's Ben's ladder!"

"Christopher, I heard you the first time. I want to know what you're doing with it."

"God! Dad! It's *Ben's ladder*. How many times do I have to tell you? It's *Ben's ladder*."

To get to the main roof, you climbed a long, sturdy down-spout near the music rooms, crossed a plain of tar and caramel-brown Missouri gravel, and climbed a metal staircase and a sheer eight-foot wall. Unless you were me, you also had to stop and drag me up the eight-foot wall. The growth spurt I'd had the year before had made me taller and heavier and clumsier, while leaving unaltered my pitiful arm and shoulder strength.

I was probably nobody's idea of an ideal fellow gang member, but I came with Manley and Davis, my old friends, who were good athletes and avid climbers of public buildings. In junior high, Manley had broken the school record for pull-ups, doing twenty-three of them. As for Davis, he'd been a football halfback and a starting basketball forward and was unbelievably tough. Once, on a January campout in a deserted Missouri state park, on a morning so cold we split our frozen grapefruits with a hatchet and fried them on an open fire (we were in a phase of cook-it-yourself fruitarianism), we found an old car hood with a towrope attached to it, irresistible, irresistible. We tied the rope to our friend Lunte's Travelall, and Lunte drove at ill-considered speeds along the unplowed park roads, towing Davis while I kept watch from the back seat. We were doing about 40 when the road plunged unexpectedly down a hill. Lunte had to brake hard and steer into a skid to avoid rolling the Travelall, which cracked the towrope like a whip and flung Davis at a sick-making velocity toward a line of heavy-duty picnic tables stacked up in falling-domino formation. It was the kind of collision that killed people. There was a sunlit explosion of sparkling powder and shattered lumber, and through the rear window, as the snow settled and Lunte slowed the vehicle, I saw Davis come trotting after us, limping a little and clutching a jagged shard of picnic table. He was shouting, he said later, "I'm alive! I'm alive!" He'd demolished one of the frozen tables— knocked it into a hundred pieces—with his ankle.

Also dragged to the roof, along with me, were the stepladder, lots of rope, two bald steel-belted radials, and the Device that Davis and I had built. Leaning out over the balustrade, we could sort of almost *touch* the flagpole. The object of our fixation wasn't more than twelve feet away from us, but its skin of aluminum paint matched the cloudy bright suburban sky behind it, and it was curiously hard to see. It seemed at once close and far away and disembodied and very accessible. The six of us stood there wishing we could touch it, groaning and exclaiming with desire to touch it.

Although Davis was a better mechanic, I was more facile than he at arguing for doing things my way. As a result, little we built ever worked. Certainly our Device, as soon became apparent, had no chance. At the end of the board was a crude wooden bracket that could never have gripped the flagpole, especially under the added weight of a tire; there was also the more fundamental difficulty of leaning out over a balustrade and pulling hard on a heavy board to control it while also trying to push it against a flagpole that, when bumped, clanged and swung distressingly. We were lucky not to send the Device through one of the windows on the floors below us. The group verdict was swift and harsh: *piece of shit*.

I laughed and said it, too: *piece of shit*. But I went off to one side, my throat thick with disappointment, and stood alone while everybody else tried the lasso. Peppel was swinging his hips like a rodeo man.

"Yee haw!"

"John-Boy, gimme that lasso."

"Yee haw!"

Over the balustrade I could see the dark trees of Webster Groves and the more distant TV-tower lights that marked the boundaries of my childhood. A night wind coming across the football practice field carried the smell of thawed winter earth, the great sorrowful world-smell of being alive beneath a sky. In my imagination, as in the pencil drawings I'd made, I'd seen the

Device work brilliantly. The contrast between the brightness of my dreams and the utter botch of my executions, the despair into which this contrast plunged me, was a recipe for self-consciousness. I felt identified with the disgraced Device. I was tired and cold and I wanted to go home.

I'd grown up amid tools, with a father who could build anything, and I thought I could do anything myself. How difficult could it be to drill a straight hole through a piece of wood? I would bear down with the utmost concentration, and the drill bit would emerge in a totally wrong place on the underside of the wood, and I would be shocked. Always. Shocked. In tenth grade I set out to build from scratch a refracting telescope with an equatorial mount and tripod, and my father, seeing the kind of work I was doing, took pity on me and built the entire thing himself. He cut threads in iron pipe for the mounting, poured concrete in a coffee can for the counterweight, hacksawed an old carbon-steel bedframe for the base of the tripod, and made a cunning lens mount out of galvanized sheet metal, machine screws, and pieces of a plastic ice-cream carton. The only part of the telescope I built on my own was the eyepiece holder, which was the only part that didn't work right, which rendered the rest of it practically useless. And so I hated being young.

It was after one o'clock when Peppel finally threw the lasso high and far enough to capture the flagpole. I stopped sulking and joined in the general cheering. But new difficulties emerged right away. Kortenhof climbed the stepladder and tugged the lasso up to within a foot of the ball, but here it snagged on the pulley and flag cables. The only way to propel a tire over the top would be to snap the rope vigorously up and down:

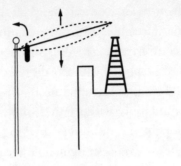

When we strung the tire out on the rope, however, it sagged out of reach of the top:

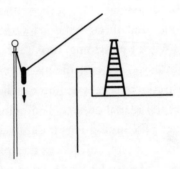

To raise the tire, Kortenhof had to pull hard on the rope, which, if you were standing on a ladder, was a good way to launch yourself over the balustrade. Four of us grabbed the ladder and applied counterforce. But this then wildly stressed the flagpole itself:

The flagpole made worrisome creaking and popping sounds as it leaned toward us. It also threatened, in the manner of a strained fishing rod, to recoil and cast Kortenhof out over Selma Avenue like a piece of bait. We were thwarted yet again. Our delight in seeing a tire rubbing up against the desired ball, nudging to within inches of the wished-for penetration, only heightened our anguish.

Two months earlier, around the time of her fifteenth birthday, my first-ever girlfriend, Merrell, had dumped me hard. She was a brainy Fellowship girl with coltish corduroy legs and straight brown hair that reached to the wallet in her back pocket. (Purses, she believed, were girly and antifeminist.) We'd come together on a church-membership retreat in a country house where I'd unrolled my sleeping bag in a carpeted closet into which Merrell and her own sleeping bag had then migrated by deliriously slow degrees. In the months that followed, Merrell had corrected my most egregious mannerisms and my most annoying misconceptions about girls, and sometimes she'd let me kiss her. We held hands through the entirety of my first R-rated movie, Lina Wertmüller's *Swept Away*, which two feminist advisors from Fellowship took a group of us to see for somewhat opaque political reasons. ("Sex but not explicit," I noted in my journal.) Then, in January, possibly in reaction to my obsessive tendencies, Merrell got busy with other friends and started avoiding me. She applied for transfer to a local private academy for the gifted and the well-to-do. Mystified, and badly hurt, I renounced what Fellowship had taught me to call the "stagnation" of romantic attachments.

Although the flagpole situation was hopeless, Kortenhof and Schroer were yanking the rope more violently, causing the pole to lurch and shudder while the worriers among us— Manley and I—told them to stop. Finally, inevitably, somebody lost hold of the rope, and we all went home with a new problem: if the rope was still in place on Monday morning, the administration would guess what we'd been up to.

Returning the next night, Saturday, we smashed the padlock at the base of the pole, released the flag cables, and tried to jostle the rope free by tugging on the cables, with no success. The once stiff rope dangled flaccidly alongside the unconquered administrative mast, its frayed end twisting in the wind, twenty feet off the ground. We came back on Sunday night with a new padlock and took turns trying to shinny up the too-thick pole, again with no success. Most of us gave up then—we may have had homework, and Schroer was heavily into *Monty Python*, which aired at eleven—but Manley and Davis returned to the school yet again and managed to release the rope by boosting each other and yanking on the cables. They put our padlock on the flagpole; and now it was our hostage.

Manley's parents were permissive, and Kortenhof's house was big enough to exit and enter inconspicuously, but most of us had trouble getting away from our parents after midnight. One Sunday morning, after two hours of sleep, I came down to breakfast and found my parents ominously untalkative. My father was at the stove frying our weekly pre-church eggs. My mother was frowning with what I now realize was probably more fear than disapproval. There was fear in her voice as well. "Dad says he heard you coming in the front door this morning after it was light," she said. "It must have been six o'clock. Were you out?"

Caught! I'd been Caught!

"Yeah," I said. "Yeah, I was over at the park with Ben and Chris."

"You said you were going to bed early. Your light was off."

"Yeah," I said, looking at the floor. "But I couldn't sleep, and they'd said they'd be over at the park, you know, if I couldn't sleep."

"What on earth were you doing out there so long?"

"Irene," my father warned, from the stove. "Don't ask the question if you can't stand to hear the answer."

"Just talking," I said.

The sensation of being Caught: it was like the buzz I once got from some cans of Reddi-wip whose gas propellent I shared with Manley and Davis—a ballooning, dizzying sensation of being all surface, my inner self suddenly so flagrant and gigantic that it seemed to force the air from my lungs and the blood from my head.

I associate this sensation with the rushing heave of a car engine, the low whoosh of my mother's Buick as it surged with alarming, incredible speed up our driveway and into our garage. It was in the nature of this whoosh that I always heard it earlier than I wanted or expected to. I was Caught privately enjoying myself, usually in the living room, listening to music, and I had to scramble.

Our stereo was housed in a mahogany-stained console of the kind sold nowadays in thrift stores. Its brand name was Aeolian, and its speakers were hidden behind doors that my mother insisted on keeping closed when she played the local all-Muzak station, KCFM, for her dinner guests; orchestral arrangements of "Penny Lane" and "Cherish" fought through cabinetry in a muffled whisper, the ornate pendent door handles buzzing with voices during KCFM's half-hourly commercial announcements. When I was alone in the house, I opened the doors and played my own records, mostly hand-me-downs from my brothers. My two favorite bands in those pre-punk years were the Grateful Dead and the Moody Blues. (My enthusiasm for the latter survived until I read, in a *Rolling Stone* review, that their music was suited to "the kind of person who whispers 'I love you' to a one-night stand.") One afternoon, I was kneeling at the Aeolian altar and playing an especially syrupy Moodies effort at such soul-stirring volume that I failed to hear my mother's automotive whoosh. She burst into the house crying, "Turn that off! That awful rock music! I can't stand it! Turn it off!" Her complaint was unjust; the song, which had no rock beat whatsoever, offered KCFMish sentiments like *Isn't life strange / A turn of the page / . . . it makes me want to cry*. But I nevertheless felt hugely Caught.

The car I preferred hearing was my father's car, the Cougar he commuted to work in, because it never showed up unexpectedly. My father understood privacy, and he was eager to accept the straight-A self that I presented to him. He was my rational and enlightened ally, the powerful engineer who helped me man the dikes against the ever-invading sea of my mother. And yet, by temperament, he was no less hostile to my adolescence than she was.

My father was plagued by the suspicion that adolescents were *getting away with something*: that their pleasures were insufficiently trammeled by conscience and responsibility. My brothers had borne the brunt of his resentment, but even with me it would sometimes boil over in pronouncements on my character. He said, "You have demonstrated a taste for expensive things, but not for the work it takes to earn them." He said, "Friends are fine, but all evening every evening is too much." He had a double-edged phrase that he couldn't stop repeating whenever he came home from work and found me reading a novel or playing with my friends: "One continuous round of pleasure!"

When I was fifteen, my Fellowship friend Hoener and I struck up a poetic correspondence. Hoener lived in a different school district, and one Sunday in the summer she came home with us after church and spent the afternoon with me. We walked over to my old elementary school and played in the dirt: made little dirt roads, bark bridges, and twig cottages on the ground beneath a tree. Hoener's friends at her school were doing the ordinary cool things—drinking, experimenting with sex and drugs—that I wasn't. I was scared of Hoener's beauty and her savoir faire and was relieved to discover that she and I shared romantic views of childhood. We were old enough not to be ashamed of playing like little kids, young enough to still become engrossed in it. By the end of our afternoon, I was close to whispering "I love you." I thought it was maybe four o'clock, but when we got back to my house we found Hoener's father waiting in his car. It was six-fifteen and he'd been waiting for an hour. "Oops," Hoener said.

Inside the house, my dinner was cold on the table. My parents (this was unprecedented) had eaten without me. My mother flickered into sight and said, "Your father has something to say to you before you sit down."

I went to the den, where he had his briefcase open on his lap. Without looking up, he announced, "You are not to see Fawn again."

"What?"

"You and she were gone for five hours. Her father wanted to know where you were. I had to tell him I had no idea."

"We were just over at Clark School."

"You will not see Fawn again."

"Why not?"

"Calpurnia is above suspicion," he said. "You are not."

Calpurnia? Suspicion?

Later that evening, after my father had cooled off, he came to my room and told me that I could see Hoener again if I wanted to. But I'd already taken his disapproval to heart. I started sending Hoener asinine and hurtful letters, and I started lying to my father as well as to my mother. Their troubles with my brother in 1970 were the kind of conflict I was bent on avoiding, and Tom's big mistake, it seemed to me, had been his failure to keep up appearances.

More and more, I maintained two separate versions of myself, the official fifty-year-old boy and the unofficial adolescent. There came a time when my mother asked me why all my undershirts were developing holes at navel level. The official version of me had no answer; the unofficial adolescent did. In 1974, crewneck white undershirts were fashion suicide, but my mother came from a world in which colored T-shirts were evidently on a moral par with water beds and roach clips, and she refused to let me wear them. Every morning, therefore, after I left the house, I pulled down my undershirt until it didn't show at the collar, and I safety-pinned it to my underpants. (Sometimes the pins opened and stuck me in the belly, but the alternative—wearing no T-shirt at all—would have made me feel too naked.) When I could get away with it, I also went to the boys' bathroom and changed out of certain grievously bad shirts. My mother, in her thrift, favored inexpensive tab-collared knits, usually of polyester, which advertised me equally as an obedient little boy and a middle-aged golfer, and which chafed my neck as if to keep me ever mindful of the shame of wearing them.

For three years, all through junior high, my social death was grossly overdetermined. I had a large vocabulary, a giddily squeaking voice, horn-rimmed glasses, poor arm strength, too-obvious approval from my teachers, irresistible urges to shout unfunny puns, a near-eidetic acquaintance with J.R.R. Tolkien, a big chemistry lab in my basement, a penchant for intimately insulting any unfamiliar girl unwise enough to speak to me, and so on. But the real cause of death, as I saw it, was my mother's refusal to let me wear jeans to school. Even my old friend Manley, who played drums and could do twenty-three pull-ups and was elected class president in ninth grade, could not afford to see me socially.

Help finally arrived in tenth grade, when I discovered Levi's straight-legged corduroys and, through the lucky chance of my Congregational affiliation, found myself at the center of the Fellowship clique at the high school. Almost overnight, I went from dreading lunch hour to happily eating at one of the crowded Fellowship tables, presided over by Peppel, Kortenhof, and Schroer. Even Manley, who was now playing drums in a band called Blue Thyme, had started coming to Fellowship meetings. One Saturday in the fall of our junior year, he called me up and asked if I wanted to go to the mall with him. I'd been planning to hang out with my science buddy Weidman, but I ditched him in a heartbeat and we never hung out again.

At lunch on Monday, Kortenhof gleefully reported that our padlock was still on the flagpole and that no flag had been raised. (It was 1976, and the high school was lax in its patriotic duties.) The obvious next step, Kortenhof said, was to form a proper group and demand official recognition. So we wrote a note—

Dear Sir,
　　We have kidnapped your flagpole. Further details later.

—made a quick decision to sign it "U.N.C.L.E." (after the sixties TV show), and delivered it to the mail slot of the high-school principal, Mr. Knight.

Mr. Knight was a red-haired, red-bearded, Nordic-looking giant. He had a sideways, shambling way of walking, with frequent pauses to hitch up his pants, and he stood with the stooped posture of a man who spent his days listening to smaller people. We knew his voice from his all-school intercom announcements. His first words—"Teachers, excuse the interruption"—often sounded strained, as if he'd been nervously hesitating at his microphone, but after that his cadences were gentle and offhanded.

What the six of us wanted, more than anything else, was to be recognized by Mr. Knight as kindred spirits, as players outside the ordinary sphere of student misbehavior and administrative force. And for a week our frustration steadily mounted, because Mr. Knight remained aloof from us, as impervious as the flagpole (which, in our correspondence, we liked to represent as personally his).

After school on Monday, we cut and pasted words and letters from magazines:

WE reSPectfuLLy dEmand THat yoU OFFiCiALLY reCoGNiZe oUR ORGaniZATion at 230 PM TuESdAy. BEGin with "TeACHers, excusE the iNTERupTIon ..." If PROperLy Done, We WiLL ReTuRN flag POLE someTiMe Wed. uNGle

The phrase "Teachers, excuse the interruption" was Manley's idea, a poke at Mr. Knight. But Manley was also worried, as was I, that the administration would crack down hard on our little group if we got a reputation for vandalism, and so we returned to school that night with a can of aluminum paint and repaired the damage we'd done to the flagpole in hammering the old lock off. In the morning, we delivered the ransom note, and two-thirty found the six of us, in our respective classrooms, unreasonably hoping that Mr. Knight would make an announcement.

Our third note was typed on a sheet of notepaper headed with a giant avocado-green HELLO:

Being as we are a brotherhood of kindly fellows, we are giving you one last chance. And observing that you have not complied with our earlier request, we are hereby reiterating it. To wit: your official recognition of our organization over the public address system at 2:59, Wednesday, March 17. If you comply, your flagpole will be returned by Thursday morning.

U.N.C.L.E.

We also made an U.N.C.L.E. flag out of a pillowcase and black electrician's tape and ran it up the flagpole under cover of night. But Mr. Knight's office didn't even notice the flag until Kortenhof casually pointed it out to a teacher—two maintenance workers were then sent outside to cut our lock with a hacksaw and lower the pirate flag—and he ignored the note. He ignored a fourth note, which offered him two dollars in compensation for the broken school padlock. He ignored a fifth note, in which we reiterated our offer and dispelled any notion that our flag had been raised in celebration of St. Patrick's Day.

By the end of the week, the only interest we'd succeeded in attracting was that of other students. There had been too much huddling and conspiring in hallways, too much blabbing on Kortenhof's part. We added a seventh member simply to buy his silence. A couple of girls from Fellowship grilled me closely: Flagpole? Uncle? Can we join?

As the whispering grew louder, and as Kortenhof developed a new plan for a much more ambitious and outstanding prank, we decided to rename ourselves. Manley, who had a half-insolent, half-genuine fondness for really stupid humor, proposed the name DIOTI. He wrote it down and showed it to me.

"An anagram for 'idiot'?"

Manley giggled and shook his head. "It's also *tio*, which is 'uncle' in Spanish, and 'di,' which means 'two.' U.N.C.L.E. Two. Get it?"

"Di-tio."

"Except it's scrambled. DIOTI sounds better."

"God, that is stupid."

He nodded eagerly, delightedly. "I know! It's so stupid! Isn't it great?"

Nine of us were piling out of two cars very late on the last Saturday of the school year, wearing dark clothes and dark stocking caps, carrying coils of rope, and zipping up knapsacks that contained hammers, wrenches, pliers, screwdrivers, and customized floor plans of the high school, when a police car rounded the corner of Selma Avenue and turned on its searchlight.

My instinct in police situations, honed by years of shooting off fireworks in a community where they were banned, was to take off running into the dark of the nearest lawn. Half of DIOTI came loping and scattering after me. It was a long time since I'd run through dark lawns uninvited. There was dew on everything, and you could encounter a dog, you could hook your foot in a croquet wicket. I stopped and hid in a group of rhododendrons where Schroer, the *Monty Python* disciple, was also hiding.

"Franzen? Is that you? You're making an incredible amount of noise."

In my knapsack, besides tools, I had Easter candy and green plastic Easter hay, five rhymed quatrains that I'd typed on slips of bond paper, and other special equipment. As my own breathing moderated, I could hear the breathing of the squad car's engine in the distance, the murmur of discussion. Then, more distinctly, a shouted whisper: "Ally-ally-out-'n'-free! Ally-ally-out-'n'-free!" The voice belonged to Holyoke, one of our new recruits, and at first I didn't understand what he was saying. The equivalent call on my own street was ally-ally-in-come-free.

"The story," Holyoke whispered as we followed him toward the patrol car, "is we're tying a door shut. Gerri Chopin's front door. We're going to the Chopins' house to tie her door shut. We're using the ropes to tie the door. And the tools are for taking off the hinges."

"Michael, that doesn't make any—"

"Why take off the hinges if we're tying—"

"Hello!"

"Hello, Officer!"

The patrolman was standing in his headlight beams, examining knapsacks, checking IDs. "This is all you have? A library card?"

"Yes, sir."

He looked in Peppel's bag. "What are you doing with such a big rope?"

"That's not a big rope," Peppel said. "That's several small ropes tied together."

There was a brief silence.

The officer asked us if we knew that it was after one o'clock.

"Yes, we do know that," Manley said, stepping forward and squaring his shoulders. He had a forthright manner whose ironic hollowness no adult, only peers, seemed able to detect.

Teachers and mothers found Manley irresistible. Certainly, in spite of his shoulder-length hair, my own mother did.

"So what are you doing out so late?"

Manley hung his head and confessed that we'd intended to tie the Chopins' screen door shut. His tone suggested that he could see now, as he couldn't five minutes ago, what a childish and negative idea this was. Standing behind him, three or four of us pointed at the Chopins' house. That's the Chopins' house right there, we said.

The officer looked at the door. We would seem to have been a rather large crew, with a lot of ropes and tools, for the task of tying one screen door shut, and we were less than a hundred yards from the high school in prime pranking season. But it was 1976 and we were white and not drunk. "Go home to bed," he said.

The squad car followed Kortenhof's station wagon back to his house, where, in his bedroom, we decided not to make a second attempt that night. If we waited until Tuesday, we could get a better cover story in place. We could say, I said, that we were observing an unusual stellar occultation by the planet Mars, and that we needed tools to assemble a telescope. I insisted that everyone memorize the bogus name of the bogus star: NGC 6346.

Luckily, the sky was clear on Tuesday night. Davis escaped his house by jumping out a window. Schroer spent the night at Peppel's and helped him push the family car out of earshot before starting it. Manley, as usual, simply got into his father's Opel and drove it to my house, where I'd climbed from my bedroom window and retrieved pieces of my hitherto useless telescope from the bushes where I'd hidden them.

"We're going to watch Mars occult NGC 6346," Manley recited.

I felt a little guilty about abusing astronomy like this, but there had always been something dubious in my relationship with nature. The official fifty-year-old enjoyed reading about science; the unofficial adolescent mostly cared about theatrics. I longed to get my hands on a bit of pure selenium or rubidium, because who else had pure selenium or rubidium in his home? But if a chemical wasn't rare, colorful, flammable, or explosively reactive, there was no point in stealing it from school. My father, my rational ally, who by his own testimony had married my mother because "she was a good writer and I thought a good writer could do anything," and who'd chafed against her romantic nature ever since, encouraged me to be a scientist and discouraged me from fancy writing. One Christmas, as a present, he built me a serious lab bench, and for a while I enjoyed imagining myself keeping a more rigorous notebook. My first and last experiment was to isolate "pure nylon" by melting a scrap of panty hose in a crucible. Turning to astronomy, I again was happy as long as I was reading books, but these books reprinted pages from amateur stargazing logs whose orderly example I couldn't follow even for one minute. I just wanted to look at pretty things.

Riding with Manley through the ghostly streets of Webster Groves, I was moved for the same reason that snow had moved me as a child, for its transformative enchantment of ordinary surfaces. The long rows of dark houses, their windows dimly reflecting streetlights, were as still as armored knights asleep under a spell. It was just as Tolkien and C. S. Lewis had promised: there really was another world. The road, devoid of cars and fading into distant haze, really did go ever on and on. Unusual things could happen when nobody was looking.

On the roof of the high school, Manley and Davis gathered ropes to rappel down exterior walls, while Kortenhof and Schroer set off for the gym, intending to enter through a high window and climb down on one of the folded-up trampolines. The rest of DIOTI went down through a trapdoor, past a crawl space, and out through a biology-department storage room.

Our floor plans showed the location of the thirty-odd bells that we'd identified while canvasing the school. Most of the bells were the size of half-coconuts and were mounted in hallways. During a lunch hour, we'd given a boost to Kortenhof, who had unscrewed the dish from one of these bells and silenced it by removing the clapper—a pencil-thick cylinder of graphite-blackened metal—from its electromagnetic housing. Two teams of two now headed off to disable the other bells and collect the clappers.

I had my slips of paper and worked alone. In a second-floor hallway, at knee level between two lockers, was an intriguing little hole with a hinged metal cap. The hole led back into obscure scholastic recesses. Manley and I had often passed idle minutes speaking into it and listening for answers.

In my laboratory at home, I'd rolled up one of my slips of paper tightly, sealed it inside a segment of glass tubing with a Bunsen flame, and tied and taped a piece of string around the tube. This ampule I now lowered through the little rabbit hole until it dropped out of sight. Then I tied the string to the hinge and shut the metal cap. On the slip of paper was a quatrain of doggerel:

> The base of a venetian blind
> Contains another clue.
> Look in the conference room that's off
> The library. (What's new?)

In the venetian blind was more doggerel that I'd planted during school hours:

> There is a clue behind the plate
> That's on the western side
> Of those large wooden fire doors
> Near room three sixty-five.

I went now and unscrewed the push plate from the fire door and taped another slip to the wood underneath:

> And last, another bookish clue
> Before the glorious find.
> *The Little Book of Bells'* the one;
> Its code is seven eight nine.

There were further quatrains hidden on an emergency-lighting fixture, rolled up inside a projection screen, and stuck in a library book called *Your School Clubs*. Some of the quatrains could have used a rewrite, but nobody thought they were a piece of shit. My idea was to enchant the school for Mr. Knight, to render the building momentarily strange and full of possibility, as a gift to him; and I was in the midst of discovering that writing was a way to do this.

During the previous two months, students from the five high-school physics classes had written and produced a farce about Isaac Newton, *The Fig Connection*. I had co-chaired the writing committee with a pretty senior girl, Siebert, toward whom I'd quickly developed strong feelings of stagnation. Siebert was a tomboy who wore bib overalls and knew how to camp, but she was also an artist who drew and wrote effortlessly and had charcoal stains and acrylic smudges on her hands, and she was also a fetching girly-girl who every so often let her hair down and wore high-waisted skirts. I wanted all of her and resented other boys for wanting any part of her. Our play was so warmly received that one of the English teachers suggested that Siebert and I try to publish it. As everything had gone wrong for me in junior high, suddenly everything was going right.

Toward three o'clock, DIOTI reconvened on the roof with booty: twenty-five clappers and five metal dishes, the latter daringly unbolted from the bigger bells that were mounted on high walls. We tied the clappers together with pink ribbon, filled the largest dish with plastic hay and Easter candy, nestled the clappers and the smaller dishes in the hay, and stashed the whole thing in the crawl space. Returning home then, Peppel and Schroer had the worst of it, pushing Peppel's car back up a hill and into his driveway. I crept back into my house less cautiously than usual. I hardly cared if I was Caught; for once, I had something they couldn't take away from me.

And to go back to school four hours later and see the place so peopled after seeing it so empty: here was a foretaste of seeing clothed in the daylight the first person you'd spent a night with naked.

And the silence then, at eight-fifteen, when the bells should have rung but didn't: this quiet transformation of the ordinary, this sound of one hand clapping, this beautiful absence, was like the poetry I wanted to learn to write.

At the end of first period, a teacher's voice came over the classroom speakers to announce that the bells were out of order. Later in the morning, the teacher began to announce not only the time but also, oddly, the temperature. Summer heat poured through the open windows, and without the usual prison-yard clanging the crowds in hallways seemed deregimented, the boundaries of the hours blurred.

Manley at lunchtime brought happy news: the reason that Mr. Knight wasn't making the announcements himself was that he was following the clues. Manley had spied him on the second floor, peering down into the rabbit hole. Despite the familiar tone we took with him, few members of DIOTI, certainly not I, had ever exchanged two words with Mr. Knight. He was the ideal, distant, benign, absurd Authority, and until now the notion that he might come out to play with us had been purely hypothetical.

The only shadow on the day was that a Device of mine again

failed to work. Davis called me after school to report that Mr. Knight had lost the glass ampule down the rabbit hole. A canny English teacher, the same one who thought our play should be published, had promised Davis anonymity in exchange for the lost clue. I recited it over the phone, and the next morning the bells were working again. Kortenhof, who had had two hundred DIOTI bumper stickers printed up, went outside with Schroer in broad daylight and applied them to every rear bumper in the faculty parking lot.

That summer my cousin Gail, my aunt and uncle's only child, was killed at the wheel of her car in West Virginia. My mother's mother was dying of liver disease in Minneapolis, and I became morbidly aware that there were fifty thousand nuclear warheads on the planet, several dozen of them targeting St. Louis. My wet dreams felt apocalyptic, like a ripping of vital organs. One night I was awakened by a violent clap of thunder and was convinced that the world was over.

It was the sweetest summer of my life. "One continuous round of pleasure," my father kept saying. I fell under the spell of Robert Pirsig and Wallace Stevens and began to write poetry. During the day, Siebert and I shot and edited a Super-8 costume drama with Davis and Lunte, and at night we painted a Rousseauian jungle mural on a wall at the high school. We were still just friends, but every evening that I spent with her was an evening that she didn't spend with other boys. On her birthday, in July, as she was leaving her house, three of us jumped her from behind, blindfolded her, tied her wrists, and put her in the back of Lunte's car. We had a surprise party waiting on a riverbank beneath an interstate overpass, and to Siebert's increasingly plaintive questions—"Jon? Chris? Guys? Is that you?"—we said nothing until Lunte did 43 in a 30 zone. The cop who pulled us over made us unblind her. When he asked her if she knew us, you could see her considering her options before she said yes.

In August, Siebert went away to college, which allowed me to idealize her from a distance, communicate mainly in writing, put energy into new theatrical projects, and casually date someone else. Late in the fall, a publisher bought *The Fig Connection* for one hundred dollars, and I told my parents I was going to be a writer. They weren't happy to hear it.

I had started keeping a journal, and I was discovering that I didn't need school in order to experience the misery of appearances. I could manufacture excruciating embarrassment in the privacy of my bedroom, simply by reading what I'd written in the journal the day before. Its pages faithfully mirrored my fraudulence and pomposity and immaturity. Reading it made me desperate to change myself, to sound less idiotic. As George Benson had stressed in *Then Joy Breaks Through*, the experiences of growth and self-realization, even of ecstatic joy, were natural processes available to believers and nonbelievers alike. And so I declared private war on stagnation and committed myself privately to personal growth. The Authentic Relationship I wanted now was with the written page.

One Sunday night at Fellowship, the group did an exercise in which it arranged itself as a continuum across the church meeting hall. One corner of the hall was designated Heart, the opposite corner Brain. As anyone could have predicted, most of the group went rushing to the Heart corner, crowding together in a warm and huggy mass. A much smaller number of people, Symes among them, scattered themselves along the center of the continuum. Way over in the Brain corner, close to nobody else, Manley and I stood shoulder to shoulder and stared back at the Heart people defiantly. It was odd to be calling myself all

Brain when my heart was so full of love for Manley. More than odd: it was hostile.

DIOTI's first prank of the new year was to batik a queen-size bedsheet and unfurl it over the school's main entrance on the morning that an accrediting committee from the North Central Association arrived to inspect the school. I built a Device involving two sheet-metal levers, a pulley, and a rope that ran across the roof and dangled by a third-floor courtyard window. When we pulled the rope on Monday morning, nothing happened. Davis had to go outside, climb to the roof in plain view, and unfurl the banner by hand. It said DIOTI WELCOMES YOU, NCA.

Through the winter, subgroups of DIOTI staged smaller side pranks. I had a taste for scenes involving costumes and toy guns. Davis and Manley kept climbing buildings, proceeding on a typical Saturday night from the gargoyled bell tower of Eden Seminary to the roofs of Washington University, and finally to the kitchen of the Presbyterian church, where freshly baked Sunday cookies were available to intruders.

For the main spring prank, we chose as a victim one of my favorite teachers, Ms. Wojak, because her room was in the middle of the second floor and had a very high ceiling, and because she was rumored to have disparaged DIOTI. It took nine of us four hours on a Wednesday night to empty thirty rooms of their desks, herd the desks downstairs and through hallways, and pack them, floor to ceiling, into Ms. Wojak's room. Some of the rooms had transoms that Manley or Davis could climb through. To get into the others, we removed the hinges from the door of the main office and made use of the keys that teachers habitually left in their mail slots. Since I was fifty as well as seventeen, I'd insisted that we take along masking tape and markers and label the desks with their room numbers before moving them, to simplify the job of putting them back. Even so, I was sorry when I saw what a violent snarl we'd made of Ms. Wojak's room. I thought she might feel singled out for persecution, and so I wrote the words CENTRALLY LOCATED on her blackboard. It was the only writing I did for DIOTI that spring. I didn't care about Mr. Knight anymore; the work was all that mattered.

During our graduation ceremonies, at the football field, the superintendent of schools told the story of the desks and cited their masking-tape labels as evidence of a "new spirit of responsibility" among young people today. DIOTI had secreted a farewell banner, batiked in school colors, in the base of the football scoreboard, but the Device I'd built to release it hadn't worked well in trials the night before, and vigilant school officials had snipped the release line before Holyoke, disguised in a fisherman's outfit and dark glasses, arrived to pull it. After the ceremony, I wanted to tell my parents that it was official: I was the author of a new spirit of responsibility among young people today. But of course I couldn't, and didn't.

I expected to start drinking and having sex that summer. Siebert had returned from college by herself (her family had moved to Texas), and we had already done some heavy stagnating on her grandmother's living-room sofa. Now Lunte and his family were about to embark on a two-month camping trip, leaving Siebert to house-sit for them. She would be in the house by herself, every night, for two months.

She and I both took jobs downtown, and on our first Friday she failed to show up for a lunch date with me. I spent the afternoon wondering whether, as with Merrell, I might be coming on too strong. But that evening, while I was eating dinner with my parents, Davis came to our house and delivered the news: Siebert was in St. Joseph's Hospital with a broken back. She'd asked Davis to take her to the top of the Eden Seminary bell tower the night before, and she'd fallen from a thirty-foot downspout.

I felt like throwing up. And yet, even as I tried to wrap my mind around the news, my most pressing concern was that my parents were getting it directly, before I could tailor it for them. I felt as if I and all my friends had been Caught in a new, large, irrevocable way. My mother, as she listened to Davis, was wearing her darkest scowl. She'd always preferred the well-spoken Manley to the lumpy Davis, and she'd never had much use for Siebert, either. Her disapproval now was radiant and total. My father, who liked Siebert, was upset nearly to the point of tears. "I don't understand what you were doing on the roof," he said.

"Yeah, well, so anyway," Davis said miserably, "so she wasn't on the roof yet. I was on the roof trying to reach down and, you know, help her."

"But, Chris, my God," my father cried. *"Why were the two of you climbing on the roof at Eden Seminary?"*

Davis looked a little pissed off. He'd done the right thing by giving me the news in person, and now, as a reward, my parents were beating up on him. "Yeah, well, so anyway," he said, "she like called me last night and she wanted me to take her up to the top of the tower. I wanted to use rope, but she's a really good climber. She didn't want the rope."

"There's a nice view from the tower," I offered. "You can see all around."

My mother turned to me severely. "Have *you* been up there?"

"No," I said, which was accidentally the truth.

"I don't understand this at all," my father said.

In Davis's Pinto, as the two of us drove to Eden, he said that he'd gone up the downspout ahead of Siebert. The downspout was solid and well anchored to the wall, and Siebert had followed him easily until she reached the gutter. If she'd just extended her hand, Davis said, he could have reached down from the roof and pulled her up. But she seemed to panic, and before he could help her the focus went out of her eyes, her hands flew back behind her head, and she went straight down, twenty-five feet, landing flat on her back on the seminary lawn. The thud, Davis said, was horrible. Without thinking, without even lowering himself off the gutter, he jumped down thirty feet and broke his fall with the roll he'd practiced after lesser jumps. Siebert was moaning. He ran and banged on the nearest lighted windows and shouted for an ambulance.

The grass at the base of the downspout was not as trampled as I'd expected. Davis pointed to the spot where the EMTs had put Siebert on a rigid pallet. I forced myself to look up at the gutter. The evening air at Eden, incoherently, was mild and delicious. There was twilight birdsong in the freshly foliated oak trees, Protestant lights coming on in Gothic windows.

"You jumped down from there?" I said.

"Yeah, it was really dumb."

Siebert, it turned out, had been fortunate in landing flat. Two of her vertebrae were shattered, but her nerves were intact. She was in the hospital for six weeks, and I went to see her every evening, sometimes with Davis, more often alone. A guitarist friend and I wrote inspirational songs and sang them for her during thunderstorms. It was dark all summer. I lay on the Luntes' pool table with rum, Löwenbräu, Seagram's, and blackberry wine in my stomach and watched the ceiling spin. I didn't hate myself, but I hated adolescence, hated the very word. In August, after Siebert's parents had taken her back to Texas with a cumbersome body brace and a lot of painkillers, I went out with the girl I'd been dating in the spring. According to my journal, we had an excellent time making out.

· · ·

Adolescence is best enjoyed without self-consciousness, but self-consciousness, unfortunately, is its leading symptom. Even when something important happens to you, even when your heart's getting crushed or exalted, even when you're absorbed in building the foundations of a personality, there come these moments when you're aware that what's happening is not the real story. Unless you actually die, the real story is still ahead of you. This alone, this cruel mixture of consciousness and irrelevance, this built-in hollowness, is enough to account for how pissed off you are. You're miserable and ashamed if you don't believe your adolescent troubles matter, but you're stupid if you do. This was the double bind from which our playing with Mr. Knight, our taking something so very useless so very seriously, had given us a miraculous fifteen-month reprieve.

But when does the real story start? At forty-five, I feel grateful almost daily to be the adult I wished I could be when I was seventeen. I work on my arm strength at the gym; I've become pretty good with tools. At the same time, almost daily, I lose battles with the seventeen-year-old who's still inside me. I eat half a box of Oreos for lunch, I binge on TV, I make sweeping moral judgments, I run around town in torn jeans, I drink martinis on a Tuesday night, I stare at beer-commercial cleavage, I define as uncool any group to which I can't belong, I feel the urge to key Range Rovers and slash their tires; I pretend I'm never going to die.

The double bind, the problem of consciousness mixed with nothingness, never goes away. You never stop waiting for the real story to start, because the only real story, in the end, is that you die. Along the way, however, Mr. Knight keeps reappearing: Mr. Knight as God, Mr. Knight as history, Mr. Knight as government or fate or nature. And the game of art, which begins as a bid for Mr. Knight's attention, eventually invites you to pursue it for its own sake, with a seriousness that redeems and is redeemed by its fundamental uselessness.

For an inexperienced Midwesterner in the fast-living East, college turned out to be a reprise of junior high. I managed to befriend a few fellow lonelyhearts, but the only pranks I was involved in were openly sadistic—pelting a popular girl with cubes of Jell-O, hauling an eight-foot length of rail into the dorm room of two better-adjusted classmates. Manley and Davis sounded no happier at their respective schools; they were smoking a lot of pot. Lunte had moved to Moscow, Idaho. Holyoke, still with DIOTI, organized a final prank involving a classroom waist-deep in crumpled newspaper.

Siebert came back to St. Louis the next summer, walking without pain, wearing clothes in the style of Annie Hall, and worked with me on a farce about a police inspector in colonial India. My feelings toward her were an adolescent stew of love-and-reconsider, of commit-and-keep-your-options-open. Manley and Davis were the ones who took me to breakfast for my birthday, on the last morning of the summer. They picked me up in Davis's car, where they also had a white cane, Davis's dimwitted spaniel, Goldie, and a pair of swimming goggles that they'd dipped in black paint. They invited me to put on the goggles, and then they gave me the cane and Goldie's leash and led me into a pancake house, where I amused them by eating a stack of pancakes like a blind man.

After breakfast, we deposited Goldie at Davis's house and went driving on arterials in the baking August heat. I guessed that our destination was the Arch, on the riverfront, and it was.

I gamely went tap-tapping through the Arch's underground lobby, my sense of hearing growing sharper by the minute. Davis bought tickets to the top of the Arch while Manley incited me to touch a Remington bronze, a rearing horse. Behind us a man spoke sharply: "Please don't touch the— Oh. Oh. I'm sorry."

I took my hands away.

"No, no, please, go ahead. It's an original Remington, but please touch it."

I put my hands back on the bronze. Manley, the little jerk, went off to giggle someplace with Davis. The park ranger's hands led mine. "Feel the muscles in the horse's chest," he urged.

I was wearing mutilated swimming goggles. My cane was a quarter-inch dowel rod with one coat of white paint. I turned to leave.

"Wait," the ranger said. "There are some really neat things I want to show you."

"Um."

He took my arm and led me deeper into the Museum of Westward Expansion. His voice grew even gentler. "How long have you been—without your sight?"

"Not long," I said.

"Feel this tepee." He directed my hand. "These are buffalo skins with the hair scraped off. Here, I'll take your cane."

We went inside the tepee, and for a daylong five minutes I dutifully stroked furs, fingered utensils, smelled woven baskets. The crime of deceiving the ranger felt more grievous with each passing minute. When I escaped from the tepee and thanked him, I was covered with sweat.

At the top of the Arch, I was finally unblinded and saw: haze, glare, coal barges, Busch Stadium, a diarrhetic river. Manley shrugged and looked at the metal floor. "We were hoping you'd be able to see more up here," he said.

It often happened on my birthday that the first fall cold front of summer came blowing through. The next afternoon, when my parents and I drove east to a wedding in Fort Wayne, the sky was scrubbed clean. Giant Illinois cornfields, nearly ripe, rippled in the golden light from behind us. You could taste, in air fresh from crossing Canada, almost everything there was to know about life around here. And how devoid of interiors the farmhouses looked in light so perfect! How impatient to be harvested the cornfields seemed in their wind-driven tossing! And how platonically green the official signs for Effingham! (Its unofficial name, I surmised, was Fuckingham.) The season had changed overnight, and I was reading better books and trying to write every day, starting over from scratch now, by myself.

My father was exceeding the speed limit by an unvarying four miles per hour. My mother spoke from the back seat. "What did you and Chris and Ben do yesterday?"

"Nothing," I said. "We had breakfast."

THE FOREIGN LANGUAGE

Man wird mich schwer davon überzeugen, daß die Geschichte des
verlorenen Sohnes nicht die Legende dessen ist, der nicht geliebt
werden wollte.*

RILKE, *Malte Laurids Brigge*

Rotwerden, Herzklopfen, ein schlechtes Gewissen: das kommt
davon, wenn man nicht gesündigt hat.[†]

KARL KRAUS

I WAS INTRODUCED to the German language by a young blond
woman, Elisabeth, whom no word smaller than "voluptuous"
suffices to describe. It was the summer I turned ten, and I was
supposed to sit beside her on the love seat on my parents' screen
porch and read aloud from an elementary German text—an un-
appetizing book about Germanic home life, with old-fashioned
Fraktur type and frightening woodcuts, borrowed from our local library—while she leaned into me, holding the book open
on my lap, and pointed to words I'd mispronounced. She was
nineteen, and her skirts were sensationally short and her little

---

*It will be difficult to persuade me that the story of the Prodigal Son is not the legend
of a person who didn't want to be loved.

†Blushing, palpitations, a guilty conscience: these are what come of not having sinned.

tops sensationally tight, and the world-eclipsing proximity of her breasts and the great southerly extent of her bare legs were intolerable to me. Sitting next to her, I felt like a claustrophobe in a crowded elevator, a person with severe restless-leg syndrome, a dental patient undergoing extended drilling. Her words, being products of her lips and tongue, carried an unwelcome intimacy, and the German language itself sounded deep-throated and wet compared to English. (How prim our "bad," how carnal their "schlecht.") I leaned away from her, but she leaned over farther, and I inched down the love seat, but she inched along after me. My discomfort was so radical that I couldn't concentrate for even one minute, and this was my only relief: most afternoons, she lost patience with me quickly.

Elisabeth was the little sister of the wife of the Austrian rail-equipment manufacturer whom my father had helped introduce to the American market. She'd come over from Vienna, at my parents' invitation, to practice her English and to experience life with an American family; she was also privately hoping to explore the new freedoms that Europeans had heard were sweeping our country. Unfortunately, these new freedoms weren't available in our particular house. Elisabeth was given my brother Bob's vacated bedroom, which looked out onto a soiled, fenced square of concrete where our neighbors' piebald hunting dog, Speckles, barked all afternoon. My mother was constantly at Elisabeth's side, taking her to lunch with her friends, to the Saint Louis Zoo, to Shaw's Garden, to the Arch, to the Muny Opera, and to Tom Sawyer's house, up in Hannibal. For relief from these loving ministrations, Elisabeth had only the company of a ten-year-old boy with freedom issues of his own.

One afternoon, on the porch, she accused me of not wanting to learn. When I denied it, she said, "Then why do you keep turning around and looking outside? Is there something out there I don't see?" I had no answer for her. I never consciously connected her body with my discomfort—never mentally formed any word like "breast" or "thigh" or "dirty," never associated her knockout presence with the schoolyard talk I'd lately started hearing ("We want two pickets to Tittsburgh, and we want the change in nipples and dimes . . ."). I only knew that I didn't like the way she made me feel, and that this was disappointing to her: she was making me a bad student, and I was making her a bad teacher. Neither of us could have been less what the other wanted. At the end of the summer, after she left, I couldn't speak a word of German.

In Chicago, where I was born, our neighbors on one side were Floyd and Dorothy Nutt. On the other side were an older couple who had a grandson named Russie Toates. The first fun I remember ever having involved putting on a new pair of red rubber boots and, incited by Russie, who was a year or two older, stomping and sliding and kicking through an enormous pile of orange-brown dog poop. The fun was memorable because I was immediately severely punished for it.

I'd just turned five when we moved to Webster Groves. On the morning of my first day of kindergarten, my mother sat me down and explained why it was important not to suck my thumb anymore, and I took her message to heart and never put thumb to mouth again, though I did later smoke cigarettes for twenty years. The first thing my friend Manley heard me say in kindergarten came in response to somebody's invitation to participate in a game. I said, "I'd rather not play."

When I was eight or nine, I committed a transgression that for much of my life seemed to me the most shameful thing I'd ever done. Late one Sunday afternoon, I was let outside after dinner and, finding no one to play with, loitered by our next-door neighbors' house. Our neighbors were still eating dinner, but I could see their two girls, one a little older than I, the other a little younger, playing in their living room while they waited for dessert to be served. Catching sight of me, they came and stood between parted curtains, looking out through a window and a storm window. We couldn't hear each other, but I wanted to entertain them, and so I started dancing, and prancing, and twirling, and miming, and making funny faces. The girls ate it up. They excited me to strike ever more extreme and ridiculous poses, and for a while I continued to amuse them, but there came a point where I could feel their attention waning, and I couldn't think of any new capers to top my old ones, and I also *could not bear* to lose their attention, and so, on an impulse—I was in a totally giddy place—I pulled my pants down.

Both girls clapped hands to their mouths in delighted mock horror. I felt instantly that there was no worse thing I could have done. I pulled up my pants and ran down the hill, past our house, to a grassy traffic triangle where I could hide among some oak trees and weather the first, worst wave of shame. In later years and decades, it seemed to me that even then, within minutes of my action, as I sat among the oak trees, I couldn't remember if I'd taken my underpants down along with my pants. This memory lapse at once tormented me and didn't matter at all. I'd been granted—and had granted the neighbor girls—a glimpse of the person I knew I was permanently in danger of becoming. He was the worst thing I'd ever seen, and I was determined not to let him out again.

Curiously shame-free, by contrast, were the hours I spent studying dirty magazines. I mostly did this after school with my friend Weidman, who had located some *Playboy*s in his parents' bedroom, but one day in junior high, while I was poking around at a construction site, I acquired a magazine of my own. Its name was *Rogue*, and its previous owners had torn out most of the pictures. The one remaining photo feature depicted a "lesbian eating orgy" consisting of bananas, chocolate cake, great volumes of whipped cream, and four dismal, lank-haired girls striking poses of such patent fakeness that even I, at thirteen, in Webster Groves, understood that "lesbian eating orgy" wasn't a concept I would ever find useful.

But pictures, even the good shots in Weidman's magazines, were a little too much for me anyway. What I loved in my *Rogue* were the stories. There was an artistic one, with outstanding dialogue, about a liberated girl named Little Charlie who tries to persuade a friend, Chris, to surrender his virginity to her; in one fascinating exchange, Chris declares (sarcastically?) that he is saving himself *for his mother*, and Little Charlie chides him: "Chris, that's sick." Another story, called "Rape—In Reverse," featured two female hitchhikers, a handgun, a devoted family man, a motel room, and a wealth of unforgettable phrases, including "'Let's get him onto the bed,'" "slurping madly," and "'Still want to be faithful to wifey?' she jeered." My favorite story was a classic about an airline stewardess, Miss Trudy Lazlo, who leans over a first-class passenger named Dwight and affords him "a generous view of her creamy white jugs," which he correctly takes to be an invitation to meet her in the first-class bathroom and have sex in various positions that I had trouble picturing exactly; in a surprise twist, the story ends with the jet's pilot pointing to a curtained recess "with a small mattress, at the back of the cockpit," where Trudy wearily lies down to service him, too. I still wasn't even hormonally capable of release from the excitement of all this, but the filthiness of *Rogue*, its absolute incompatibility with my parents, who considered me their clean little boy, made me more intensely happy than any book I ever read.

Weidman and I once forged notes from our respective mothers so that we could leave school at noon and watch the first Skylab liftoff. There was nothing either technological or scientific (except, in my case, animals) that Weidman and I didn't interest ourselves in. We set up competing chemistry labs, dabbled in model railroading, accumulated junked electronic equipment, played with tape recorders, worked as lab assistants, did joint science-fair projects, took classes at the Planetarium, wrote BASIC programs for the modem-driven computer terminal at school, and made fantastically flammable "liquid-fuel rockets" out of test tubes, rubber stoppers, and benzene. On my own, I subscribed to *Scientific American*, collected rocks and minerals, became an expert on lichens, grew tropical plants from fruit seeds, sliced stuff with a microtome and put it under a microscope, performed homemade physics experiments with springs and pendular weights, and read all of Isaac Asimov's collections of popular science writings, back to back, in three weeks. My first hero was Thomas Edison, whose adult life had consisted entirely of free time. My first stated career goal was "inventor." And so my parents assumed, not implausibly, that I would become some sort of scientist. They asked Bob, who was studying medicine, what foreign language a budding scientist ought to take in high school, and he answered unequivocally: German.

When I was seven, my parents and I had gone to visit Bob at the University of Kansas. His room was in Ellsworth Hall, a teeming high-rise with harsh lighting and a pervasive locker-room smell. Following my parents into Bob's room, I saw the centerfold on his wall just as my mother cried out, in anger and disgust, *"Bob! Bob! Oh! Ugh! I can't believe you put that on your wall!"*

Even apart from my mother's judgment, which I'd learned to fear greatly, the bloody reds of the pinup girl's mouth and areolas would have struck me as violent. It was as if the girl had been photographed emerging, skinny and raw and vicious, from a terrible accident that her own derangement had caused. I was scared and offended by what she was inflicting on me and what Bob was inflicting on our parents. "Jon can't be in this room," my mother declared, turning me toward the door. Outside, she told me that she didn't understand Bob at all.

He became more discreet after that. When we returned for his graduation, three years later, he taped a construction-paper bikini onto his current pinup girl, who in any case looked to me warm and gentle and hippieish—I liked her. Bob went on to bask in my mother's approval of his decision to come home to St. Louis and go to medical school. If there were girlfriends, I never had the pleasure of meeting them. He did, though, once, bring a med-school acquaintance home for Sunday dinner, and the friend told a story in which he mentioned lying in bed with his girlfriend. I barely even clocked this detail, but as soon as Bob was gone my mother gave me her opinion of it. "I don't know if he was trying to show off, or shock us, or act sophisticated," she said, "but if what he said about cohabiting with his girlfriend is true, then I want you to know that I think he's an immoral person and that I'm very disappointed that Bob is friends with him, because I *categorically disapprove* of that kind of lifestyle."

That kind of lifestyle was my brother Tom's. After the big fight with my father, he'd gone on to graduate from Rice in film studies and live in Houston slum houses with his artist friends. I was in tenth grade when he brought home one of these friends, a slender, dark-haired woman named Lulu, for Christmas. I couldn't look at Lulu without feeling as if my breath had been knocked out of me, she was so close to the ideal of casual mid-seventies sexiness. I agonized over what book to buy her for a Christmas present, to make her feel more welcome in the family. My mother, meanwhile, was practically psychotic with hatred. "'Lulu'? 'Lulu'? What kind of person has a name like Lulu?" She gave a creaky little laugh. "When *I* was a girl, a lulu was a crazy person! Did you know that? A *lulu* was what we called a kooky crazy person!"

A year later, when both Bob and Tom were living in Chicago and I went to see them for a weekend, my mother forbade me to stay in Tom's apartment, where Lulu also dwelt. Tom was studying film at the Art Institute, making austere non-narrative shorts with titles like "Chicago River Landscape," and my mother sensed, accurately, that he had an unhealthy degree of influence over me. When Tom made fun of Cat Stevens, I removed Cat Stevens from my life. When Tom gave me his Grateful Dead LPs, the Dead became my favorite band, and when he cut his hair and moved on to Roxy Music and Talking Heads and DEVO, I cut my hair and followed. Seeing that he bought his clothes at Amvets, I started shopping at thrift stores. Because he lived in a city, I wanted to live in a city; because he made his own yogurt with reconstituted milk, I wanted to make my own yogurt with reconstituted milk; because he took notes in a six-by-nine-inch ring binder, I bought a six-by-nine-inch ring binder and started a journal in it; because he made movies of industrial ruins, I bought a camera and took pictures of industrial ruins; because he lived hand to mouth and did carpentry and rehabbed apartments with scavenged materials, hand to mouth was the way I wanted to live, too. The hopelessly unattainable goddesses of my late adolescence were the art-school girls who orbited Tom in their thrift-store clothes and spiky haircuts.

. . .

There was nothing cool about high-school German. It was the language that none of my friends were taking, and the sun-faded tourist posters in the room of the German teacher, Mrs. Fares, were not a persuasive argument for visiting Germany or falling for its culture. (This much was true of the French and Spanish rooms as well. It was as if the modern languages were so afraid of adolescent scorn that even the classrooms were forced to dress predictably—to wear posters of the bullfight, the Eiffel Tower, the castle Neuschwanstein.) Many of my classmates had German parents or grandparents, whose habits ("He likes his beer warm") and traditions ("We have Lebkuchen at Christmas") were of similarly negligible interest to me. The language itself, though, was a snap. It was all about memorizing four-by-four matrixes of adjective endings, and following rules. It was about grammar, which was the thing I was best at. Only the business of German gender, the seeming arbitrariness of *the* spoon and *the* fork and *the* knife,* gave me fits.

Even as the bearded Mutton and his male disciples were re-capitulating old patriarchies, Fellowship was teaching us to question our assumptions about gender roles. Boys were praised and rewarded for shedding tears, girls for getting mad and swear-ing. The weekly Fellowship "women's group" became so popu-lar that it had to be split in two. One female advisor invited girls to her apartment and gave vivid tutorials in how to have sex and not get pregnant. Another advisor challenged the patriarchy so needlingly that once, when she asked Chip Jahn to talk about his feelings, he replied that he felt like dragging her out to the parking lot and beating the shit out of her. For parity, two male advisors tried to start a men's group, but the only boys who

Der (masculine) Löffel; *die* (feminine) Gabel; *das* (neuter) Messer.

joined it were the already-sensitized ones who wished they could belong to the women's group.

Being a woman seemed to me the happening thing, compared to being a man. From the popularity of the weekly support groups, I gathered that women truly had been oppressed and that we men therefore ought to defer to them, and be nurturing and supportive, and cater to their wishes. It was especially important, if you were a man, to look deep into your heart and make sure you weren't objectifying a woman you loved. If even a tiny part of you was exploiting her for sex, or putting her on a pedestal and worshipping her, this was very bad.

In my senior-year journal, while I waited for Siebert to return from her first year of college, I constantly policed my feelings about her. I wrote "Don't CANONIZE her" and "*Don't be in love* or anything idiotically destructive like that" and "Jealousy is characteristic of a possessive relationship" and "*We are not sacred.*" When I caught myself writing her name in block letters, I went back and annotated: "Why the hell capitalize it?" I ridiculed and reviled my mother for her dirty-mindedness in thinking I cared about sex. I did, while Siebert was away, date a racy Catholic girl, O., who taught me to enjoy the raw-cauliflower aftertaste of cigarettes in a girl's mouth, and I did casually assume that Siebert and I would be losing our virginity before I had to leave for college. But I imagined this loss as a grown-up and serious and friendship-affirming thing, not as intercourse of the kind I'd read about in *Rogue*. I'd finished with sex like that in junior high.

One summer evening, soon after Siebert broke her back, just before I turned eighteen, my friends Holyoke and Davis and I were painting a mural, and Holyoke asked Davis and me how often we masturbated. Davis answered that he didn't do that anymore. He said he'd tried it a few times, but he'd decided it wasn't really something he enjoyed.

Holyoke looked at him with grave astonishment. "You didn't enjoy it."

"No, not really," Davis said. "I wasn't that into it."

Holyoke frowned. "Do you mind if I ask what . . . technique . . . and materials . . . you were using?"

I listened carefully to the discussion that ensued, because, unlike Davis, I hadn't even tried it.

The first-year German teacher at Swarthmore College was a flamboyant, elastic-mouthed one-man show, Gene Weber, who pranced and swooped and slapped desktops and addressed his first-year students as "bambini." He had the manner of an inspired, witty preschool teacher. He found everything in his classroom hilarious, and if the bambini couldn't generate hilarity themselves, he said hilarious things for them and laughed on their behalf. I didn't dislike Weber, but I resisted him. The teacher I adored was the drill instructor, Frau Plaxton, a woman of limitless patience and beautifully chiseled Nordic looks. I saw her every Tuesday and Thursday at 8:30 a.m., an hour made tolerable by her affectionate, bemused way of saying "Herr Franzen" when I walked into the room. No matter how badly her students had prepared, Frau Plaxton couldn't frown sternly without also smiling at her sternness. The German vowels and consonants she overpronounced for heuristic purposes were as juicy as good plums.

On the other weekdays at 8:30, I had Several-Variable Calculus, a freshman class designed to winnow out students whose devotion to math/science was less than fanatical. By spring break, I was in danger of failing it. If I'd intended to pursue a career in science—as the official fifty-year-old continued to assure his parents that he did—I should have spent my spring break catching up. Instead, my friend Ekström and I took a bus from Philadelphia to

Houston so that I could see Siebert, who was out of her back brace and living in a dorm at the University of Houston.

One night, to get away from her roommate, she and I went outside and sat on a bench in a courtyard surrounded by concrete walls. Siebert told me that one of her teachers, the poet Stephen Spender, had been talking a lot about Sigmund Freud, and that she'd been thinking about her fall from the downspout at Eden Seminary a year earlier. The night before she'd fallen, she and our friend Lunte had been hanging out at my house, and the doorbell had rung, and before I knew what was happening, Siebert was meeting my former sort-of girlfriend, O., for the first time. O. was with Manley and Davis, who had just taken her up to the top of the Eden Seminary bell tower. She was flushed and beaming from the climb, and she didn't mind admitting that Manley and Davis had tied ropes around her and basically dragged her up the downspout; her physical unfitness was something of a joke.

Siebert had lost all memory of the day after she met O., but other people had subsequently told her what she'd done. She'd called up Davis and said she wanted to climb the same tower that O. had climbed. When Davis suggested that Manley come along, or that they at least take a rope, Siebert said no, she didn't need Manley and she didn't need ropes. And, indeed, she hadn't had any trouble climbing up the downspout. It was only at the top, while Davis was reaching down to help her past the gutter, that she'd thrown back her hands. And Freud, she told me, had a theory of the Unconscious. According to Stephen Spender, who had a way of singling her out and fastening his uncanny blue eyes on her whenever he spoke of it, Freud believed that when you made a strange mistake, the conscious part of you believed it was an accident, but in fact it was never an accident: you were doing exactly what the dark, unknowable part of you wanted to do. When your hand slipped and you cut yourself with a knife, it was because the hidden part of you wanted you to cut yourself. When you said "my mother" instead of "my wife," it was because your id really did mean "my mother." Siebert's post-traumatic amnesia was total, and it was hard to imagine anyone less suicidal than her; but what if she'd *wanted* to fall off the roof? What if the Unconscious in her had wanted to die, because of my dalliance with O.? What if, at the top of the downspout, she'd ceased to be herself and become entirely that dark, other thing?

I'd heard of Freud, of course. I knew that he was Viennese and important. But his books had looked unpleasant and forbidding whenever I'd pulled one off a shelf, and until this moment I'd managed to know almost nothing about him. Siebert and I sat silently in the deserted concrete courtyard, breathing the vernal air. The loosenings of spring, the fragrances of breeding, the letting go, the thaw, the smell of warm mud: it was no longer as dreadful to me as it had been when I was ten. It was delicious now, too. But also still somewhat dreadful. Sitting in the courtyard and thinking about what Siebert had said, confronting the possibility that I, too, had an Unconscious that knew as much about me as I knew little about it, an Unconscious always looking for some way out of me, some way to escape my control and do its dirty work, to pull my pants down in front of the neighbor girls, I started screaming in terror. I screamed at the top of my lungs, which freaked both me and Siebert out. Then I went back to Philadelphia and put the whole episode out of my mind.

My instructor for third-semester intensive German was the other tenured professor in the department, George Avery, a nervous, handsome, scratchy-voiced Greek-American who seemed hard-pressed to speak in sentences shorter than three hundred words. The grammar we were supposed to review didn't greatly interest Avery. On the first day of class, he looked at his materials, shrugged, said, "I'm guessing you're all familiar with this," and embarked on a rambling digression about colorful and seldom-heard German idioms. The following week, twelve of the fourteen students in the class signed a petition in which they threatened to quit unless Avery was removed and replaced with Weber. I was against the petition—I thought it was mean to embarrass a professor, even if he was nervous and hard to follow, and I didn't miss being called a bambino—but Avery was duly yanked and Weber came prancing back.

Since I'd nearly flunked Several-Variable Calculus, I had no future in hard science, and since my parents had suggested I might want to pay for college myself if I insisted on being an English major, I was left with German by default. Its main attraction as a major was that I got easy A's in it, but I assured my parents that I was preparing myself for a career in international banking, law, diplomacy, or journalism. Privately, I looked forward to spending my junior year abroad. I wasn't liking college much—it was a comedown from high school in every way—and I was still technically a virgin, and I was counting on Europe to fix that.

But I couldn't seem to catch a break. The summer before I left for Europe, I inquired about an odd, lanky beauty I'd once danced with in a high-school gym class and had been fantasizing about at college, but she turned out to have a boyfriend and a heroin habit now. I went on two dates with Manley's younger sister, who surprised me on the second date by bringing along a chaperone, her friend MacDonald, who'd thought I was a cheater. I went off to study German literature in Munich, and on my third night there, at a party for new students, I met a lucid, pretty Bavarian girl who suggested that we go have a drink. I replied that I was tired but it might be nice to see her some other time. I never saw her again. The ratio of male students to female students in Munich's dorms was 3:1. During the next ten months, I met not one other interesting German girl who gave me the time of day. I cursed my terrible luck in having been given my only chance so early in the year. If I'd been in Munich even just a week longer, I told myself, I might have played things differently and landed a terrific girlfriend and become totally fluent in German. Instead, I spoke a lot of English with American girls. I contrived to spend four nights in Paris with one of them, but she turned out to be so inexperienced that even kissing was scary for her: unbelievably bad luck. I went to Florence, stayed in a hotel that doubled as a brothel, and was surrounded in three dimensions by people industriously fucking. On a trip to rural Spain, I had a Spanish girlfriend for a week, but before we could learn each other's languages I had to go back to stupid Germany and take exams: just my luck. I pursued a more promisingly jaded American, sat and drank and smoked with her for hours, listened to "London Calling" over and over, and tested what I believed were the outer limits of pushiness compatible with being a nurturing and supportive male. I lived in daily expectation of scoring, but in the end, after months of pursuit, she decided she was still in love with her Stateside ex. Alone in my dorm room, I could hear multiple neighbors humping—my walls and ceiling were like amplifiers. I transferred my affections to yet another American, this one with a rich German boyfriend whom she bossed around and then bemoaned behind his back. I thought if I listened long enough to her complaints about the boyfriend, and helped her realize what an unsupportive and unnurturing asshole he was, she would come to her senses and choose me. But my bad luck was beyond belief.

· · ·

Without the distraction of a girlfriend, I did learn a lot of German in Munich. Goethe's poetry particularly infected me. For the first time in my life, I was smitten with a language's mating of sound and sense. There was, for example, all through *Faust*, the numinous interplay of the verbs *streben*, *schweben*, *weben*, *leben*, *beben*, *geben**—six trochees that seemed to encapsulate the inner life of an entire culture. There were insane German gushings, like these words of thanks that Faust offers Nature after a really good night's sleep—

> Du regst und rührst ein kräftiges Beschließen
> Zum höchsten Dasein immerfort zu streben†

—which I endlessly repeated to myself, half in jest and half adoringly. There was the touching and redeeming German yearning not to be German at all but to be Italian instead, which Goethe captured in his classic verse in *Wilhelm Meister*:

> Kennst du das Land wo die Zitronen blühn,
> Im dunkeln Laub die Goldorangen glühn . . .
> Kennst du es wohl?‡

There were other lines that I recited every time I climbed a church tower or walked to the top of a hill, lines uttered by Faust after cherubs have wrested his spirit from the Devil's clutches and installed him in Heaven:

---

*Strive, float, weave, live, tremble, give.

†You awaken and stir a powerful resolve / To strive, henceforth, for the highest form of being.

‡Do you know the country where the lemon trees bloom, / and the oranges like gold in leafy gloom . . . Maybe you know it?

Hier ist die Aussicht frei,
Der Geist erhoben.
Dort ziehen Frauen vorbei,
Schwebend nach oben*

There were even, in *Faust*, short passages in which I recognized an actual emotion of my own, as when our hero, trying to settle down to work in his study, hears a knocking on his door and cries out in exasperation, "Wer plagt mich jetzt?"[†]

But despite my pleasure at feeling a language take root in me, and despite the tightly reasoned term papers I was writing on Faust's relationship with Nature and Novalis's relationship with mines and caves, I still saw literature as basically just the game I had to master in order to get a college degree. Reciting from *Faust* on windy hilltops was a way of indulging but also defusing and finally making fun of my own literary yearnings. Real life, as I understood it, was about marriage and success, not the blue flower. In Munich, where students could buy standing-room theater seats for five marks, I went to see a big-budget production of Part II of *Faust*, and on my way out of the theater I heard a middle-aged man snickeringly offer his wife this "complete and sufficient" summary of the play: "Er geht von einer Sensation zur anderen—aber keine Befriedigung."[‡] The man's disrespect, his philistine amusement with himself, amused me, too.

The German department's difficult professor, George Avery, taught the seminar in German modernism that I took in my last

---

*Here the view is clear, / The spirit exalted. / Over there, moving past, / Women float skyward.

[†]"Who's bothering me now?"

[‡]"He goes from one sensation to another—but no satisfaction."

fall at college. Avery had dark Greek eyes, beautiful skin, a strong nose, luxuriant eyebrows. His voice was high and perpetually hoarse, and when he got lost in the details of a digression, as often happened, the noise of his hoarseness overwhelmed the signal of his words. His outbursts of delighted laughter began at a frequency above human hearing—a mouth thrown open silently—and descended through an accelerating series of cries: "Hah!   Hah!   Hah!   Hah! Hah! Hah!" His eyes gleamed with excitement and pleasure if a student said anything remotely pertinent or intelligent; but if the student was altogether wrong, as the six of us in his seminar often were, he flinched and scowled as if a bug were flying at his face, or he gazed out a window unhappily, or refilled his pipe, or wordlessly cadged a cigarette from one of us smokers, and hardly even pretended to listen. He was the least polished of all my college teachers, and yet he had something that the other teachers didn't have: he felt for literature the kind of headlong love and gratitude that a born-again Christian feels for Jesus. His highest praise for a piece of writing was "It's *crazy!*" His yellowed, disintegrating copies of German prose masterworks were like missionary Bibles. On page after page, each sentence was underscored or annotated in Avery's microscopic handwriting, illuminated with the cumulative appreciations of fifteen or twenty rereadings. His paperbacks were at once low-priced, high-acid crapola and the most precious of relics—moving testaments to how full of significance every line in them could be to a student of their mysteries, as every leaf and sparrow in Creation sings of God to the believer.

Avery's father was a Greek immigrant who'd worked as a waiter and later owned a shoe-repair shop in North Philadelphia. Avery had been drafted into the Army as an eighteen-year-old, in 1944, and at the end of basic training, in the middle of the night before his unit shipped out to Europe, his commanding officer shook him roughly and shouted, "Avery! Wake up! YOUR MOTHER'S DEAD." Granted leave to attend her funeral, Avery reached Europe two weeks late, arriving on V-Day, and never caught up with his regiment. He was passed along from unit to unit and eventually landed in Augsburg, where the Army put him to work at a requisitioned publishing house. One day, his commander asked if anyone in the unit wanted to take a course in journalism. Avery was the only one who volunteered, and over the next year and a half he taught himself German, went around in civilian clothes, reported on music and art for the occupation newspaper, and fell in love with German culture. Returning to the States, he studied English and then German literature, which was how he'd ended up married to a beautiful Swiss woman and tenured at a fancy college and living in a three-story house in whose dining room, every Monday afternoon at four, we took a break for coffee and pastry that his wife, Doris, made for us.

The Averys' taste in china, furniture, and room temperature was Continental modern. As we sat at their table, speaking German with varying degrees of success, drinking coffee that went cold in five seconds, the leaves I saw scattering across the front lawn could have been German leaves, blown by a German wind, and the rapidly darkening sky a German sky, full of autumn weltschmerz. Out in the hallway, the Averys' dog, Ina, an apologetic-looking German shepherd, shivered herself awake. We weren't fifteen miles from the tiny row house where Avery had grown up, but the house he lived in now, with its hardwood floors and leather upholstery and elegant ceramics (many of them thrown by Doris, who was a skilled potter), was the kind of place I now wished I'd grown up in myself, an oasis of fully achieved self-improvement.

We read Nietzsche's *Birth of Tragedy*, stories by Schnitzler and Hofmannsthal, and a novel by Robert Walser that made me want to scream, it was so quiet and subtle and bleak. We read an essay by Karl Kraus, "The Chinese Wall," about a Chinese laundry owner in New York who sexually serviced well-bred Caucasian women and finally, notoriously, strangled one of them. The essay began, "Ein Mord ist geschehen, und die Menschheit möchte um Hilfe rufen"*—which seemed to me a little strong. The Chinatown murder, Kraus continued, was "the most important event" in the two-thousand-year history of Christian morality: also a bit strong, no? It took me half an hour to fight through each page of his allusions and alliterative dichotomies—

> Da entdecken wir, daß unser Verbot ihr Vorschub, unser Geheimnis ihre Gelegenheit, unsere Scham ihr Sporn, unser Gefahr ihr Genuß, unsere Hut ihre Hülle, unser Gebet ihre Brust war . . . [D]ie gefesselte Liebe liebte die Fessel, die geschlagene den Schmerz, die beschmutzte den Schmutz. Die Rache des verbannten Eros war der Zauber, allen Verlust in Gewinn zu wandeln.†

—and as soon as I was sitting in Avery's living room, attempting to discuss the essay, I realized that I'd been so busy deciphering Kraus's sentences that I hadn't actually read them. When Avery asked us what the essay was about, I flipped through my xeroxed pages and tried to speed-read my way to some plausible summary. But Kraus's German opened up only to lovers with a very slow hand. "It's about," I said, "um, Christian morality . . . and—"

---

*A murder has occurred, and mankind would like to cry for help.

†Now we find out that our prohibitions were Nature's procrastinations, our secrets her opportunities, our shame her spur, our danger her enjoyment, our defenses her cover, our prayers her breeding season . . . Fettered love loved its fetters; beaten love, its pain; filthy love, its filth. The revenge of the exiled Eros was the magic of turning every loss into a gain.

Avery cut me off as if I hadn't spoken. *"We like sex dirty,"* he said with a leer, looking at each of us in turn. *"That's* what this is about. The dirtier Western culture makes it, the more we like it dirty."

I was irritated by his "we." My understanding of sex was mainly theoretical, but I was pretty sure I didn't like it dirty. I was still looking for a lover who was, first and foremost, a friend. For example: the dark-haired, ironic French major who was taking the modernism seminar with me and whom I'd begun to pursue with the passive, low-pressure methods that, although they'd invariably failed me in the past, I continued to place my faith in. I'd heard that the French major was unattached, and she seemed to find me amusing. I couldn't imagine anything dirty about having sex with her. In fact, in spite of my growing preoccupation with her, I never came close to picturing us having sex of any kind.

The previous summer, to prepare for the seminar, I'd read Rilke's novel, *The Notebooks of Malte Laurids Brigge*. It immediately became my all-time favorite book, which was to say that there were several paragraphs in the first part of it (the easiest part and the only part I'd completely enjoyed) which I'd taken to reading aloud to impress my friends. The plot of the novel— a young Danish guy from a good family washes up in Paris, lives hand to mouth in a noisy rooming house, gets lonely and weirded out, worries about becoming a better writer and a more complete person, goes for long walks in the city, and otherwise spends his time writing in his journal—seemed highly relevant and interesting to me. I memorized, without ever quite grasping what I was memorizing, several passages in which Malte reports on his personal growth, which reminded me pleasantly of my own journals:

Ich lerne sehen. Ich weiß nicht, woran es liegt, es geht alles tiefer in mich ein und bleibt nicht an der Stelle stehen, wo es sonst immer zu Ende war. Ich habe ein Inneres, von dem ich nicht wußte. Alles geht jetzt dorthin. Ich weiß nicht, was dort geschieht.*

I also liked Malte's very cool descriptions of his new subjectivity in action, such as:

Da sind Leute, die tragen ein Gesicht jahrelang, natürlich nutzt es sich ab, es wird schmutzig, es bricht in den Falten, es weitet sich aus wie Handschuhe, die man auf der Reise getragen hat. Das sind sparsame, einfache Leute; sie wechseln es nicht, sie lassen es nicht einmal reinigen.†

But the sentence in *Malte* that became my motto for the semester was one I didn't notice until Avery pointed it out to us. It's spoken to Malte by a friend of his family, Abelone, when Malte is a little boy and is reading aloud thoughtlessly from Bettina von Arnim's letters to Goethe. He starts to read one of Goethe's replies to Bettina, and Abelone cuts him off impatiently. "Not the answers," she says. And then she bursts out, "Mein Gott, was hast du schlecht gelesen, Malte."‡

This was essentially what Avery said to the six of us when we were halfway through our first discussion of *The Trial*. I'd been

---

*I'm learning to see. I don't know why it is, but everything penetrates into me more deeply and doesn't stop at the place where, until now, it always used to end. I have an inner life that I didn't know about. Everything goes there now. I don't know what happens there.

†There are people who wear the same face for years, naturally it gets worn out, it gets dirty, it splits at the folds, it stretches like a pair of gloves that you've worn on a trip. These are thrifty, simple people; they don't change their face, they never even have it cleaned.

‡"My God, how badly you've been reading, Malte."

unusually quiet that week, hoping to conceal my failure to read the second half of the novel. I already knew what the book was about—an innocent man, Josef K., caught up in a nightmarish modern bureaucracy—and it seemed to me that Kafka piled on far too many examples of bureaucratic nightmarishness. I was annoyed as well by his reluctance to use paragraph breaks, and by the irrationality of his storytelling. It was bad enough that Josef K. opens the door of a storage room at his office and finds a torturer beating two men, one of whom cries out to K. for help. But to have K. return to the storage room the next night and find exactly the same three men doing exactly the same thing: I felt sore about Kafka's refusal to be more realistic. I wished he'd written the chapter in some friendlier way. It seemed like he was being a bad sport somehow. Although Rilke's novel was impenetrable in places, it had the arc of a Bildungsroman and ended optimistically. Kafka was more like a bad dream I wanted to stop having.

"We've been talking about this book for two hours," Avery said to us, "and there's a very important question that nobody is asking. Can someone tell me what the obvious important question is?"

We all just looked at him.

"*Jonathan*," Avery said. "You've been very quiet this week."

"Well, you know, the nightmare of the modern bureaucracy," I said. "I don't know if I have much to say about it."

"You don't see what this has to do with your life."

"Less than with Rilke, definitely. I mean, it's not like I've had to deal with a police state."

"But Kafka's about your life!" Avery said. "Not to take anything away from your admiration of Rilke, but I'll tell you right now, Kafka's a lot more about your life than Rilke is. Kafka was like *us*. All of these writers, they were human beings trying to make sense of their lives. But Kafka above all! Kafka was afraid of death, he had problems with sex, he had problems with women, he had problems with his job, he had problems with his parents. And he was writing fiction to try to figure these things out. *That's* what this book is about. That's what all of these books are about. Actual living human beings trying to make sense of death and the modern world and the mess of their lives."

Avery then called our attention to the book's title in German, *Der Prozeß*, which means both "the case" and "the process." Citing a text from our secondary-reading list, he began to mumble about three different "universes of interpretation" in which the text of *The Trial* could be read: one universe in which K. is an innocent man falsely accused, another universe in which the degree of K.'s guilt is undecidable . . . I was only half listening. The windows were darkening, and it was a point of pride with me never to read secondary literature. But when Avery arrived at the third universe of interpretation, in which Josef K. is *guilty*, he stopped and looked at us expectantly, as if waiting for us to get some joke; and I felt my blood pressure spike. I was offended by the mere mention of the possibility that K. was guilty. It made me feel frustrated, cheated, injured. I was outraged that a critic was allowed even to suggest a thing like that.

"Go back and look at what's on the page," Avery said. "Forget the other reading for next week. You have to read what's on the page."

Josef K., who has been arrested at home on the morning of his thirtieth birthday, returns to his rooming house after a long day at work and apologizes to his landlady, Frau Grubach, for the morning's disturbances. The arresting officials briefly commandeered the room of another boarder, a young woman named

Bürstner, but Frau Grubach assures K. that her room has been put back in order. She tells K. not to worry about his arrest—it's not a criminal matter, thank God, but something very "learned" and mysterious. K. says he "agrees" with her: the matter is "completely null and void." He asks Frau Grubach to shake his hand to seal their "agreement" about how meaningless it is. Frau Grubach instead replies, with tears in her eyes, that he shouldn't take the matter so much to heart. K. then casually asks about Fräulein Bürstner—is she home yet? He has never exchanged more than hellos with Fräulein Bürstner, he doesn't even know her first name, but when Frau Grubach confides that she worries about the men Fräulein Bürstner is hanging out with and how late she's been coming home, K. becomes "enraged." He declares that he knows Fräulein Bürstner *very well* and that Frau Grubach is *completely mistaken* about her. He angrily goes into his room, and Frau Grubach hastens to assure him that her only concern is with the moral purity of her rooming house. To which K., through a chink in the door, bizarrely cries, "If you want to keep your rooming house clean, you'd better start by asking me to leave!" He shuts the door in Frau Grubach's face, ignores her "faint knocking," and proceeds to lie in ambush for Fräulein Bürstner.

He has no particular desire for the girl—can't even remember what she looks like. But the longer he waits for her, the angrier he gets. Suddenly it's *her* fault that he skipped his dinner and his weekly visit to a B-girl. When she finally comes in, toward midnight, he tells her that he's been waiting more than two and a half hours (this is a flat-out lie), and he insists on having a word with her immediately. Fräulein Bürstner is so tired she can hardly stand up. She wonders aloud how K. can accuse her of being "late" when she had no idea he was even waiting for her. But she agrees to talk for a few minutes in her room. Here K. is excited to learn that Fräulein Bürstner has some training as a legal secretary; he says, "That's excellent, you'll be able to help me with my case." He gives her a detailed account of what happened in the morning, and when he senses that she's insufficiently impressed with his story, he starts moving her furniture around and reenacting the scene. He mentions, for no good reason, that a blouse of hers was hanging on the window in the morning. Impersonating the arresting officer, who was actually quite polite and soft-spoken, he screams his own name so loudly that another boarder knocks on Fräulein Bürstner's door. She tries again to get rid of K.—he's now been in her room for half an hour, and she has to get up very early in the morning. But he won't leave her alone. He assures her that, if the other boarder makes trouble for her, he'll personally vouch for her respectability. In fact, if need be, he'll tell Frau Grubach that everything was his fault—that he "assaulted" her in her bedroom. And then, as Fräulein Bürstner tries yet again to get rid of him, he really does assault her:

> . . . lief vor, faßte sie, küßte sie auf den Mund und dann über das ganze Gesicht, wie ein durstiges Tier mit der Zunge über das endlich gefundene Quellwasser hinjagt. Schließlich küßte er sie auf den Hals, wo die Gurgel ist, und dort ließ er die Lippen lange liegen.*

"Now I'll go," he says, wishing he knew her first name. Fräulein Bürstner nods tiredly and walks away with her head down and her shoulders slumping. Before he falls asleep, K. thinks about his behavior with her and concludes that he's pleased with it—indeed, is surprised only that he's not even more pleased.

I thought I'd read every word of the first chapter of *The Trial*

---

*. . . rushed over, grabbed her, kissed her on the mouth and then all over her face, the way a thirsty animal works its tongue over the long-sought spring water. Finally he kissed her neck, where the throat is, and let his lips lie there a long time.

twice, in German and in English, but when I went back now I realized that I'd never read the chapter even once. What was actually on the page, as opposed to what I'd expected to find there, was so unsettling that I'd shut my mind down and simply made believe that I was reading. I'd been so convinced of the hero's innocence that I'd missed what the author was saying, clearly and unmistakably, in every sentence. I'd been blind the way K. himself is blind. And so, disregarding Avery's talk of three universes of interpretive possibility, I became dogmatically attached to the opposite of my original supposition. I decided that K. is a creepy, arrogant, selfish, abusive shmuck who, because he refuses to examine his life, is having it forcibly examined for him.

That fall, I was happier than I'd been since high school. My friend Ekström and I were living in a two-room double in a centrally located dorm, and I'd lucked into the job of editing the college literary magazine. In the same zany early-seventies spirit that had saddled the college's art-film series with the name TAFFOARD,* the magazine was called *The Nulset Review*. Its previous editor was a petite red-haired poet from New York who'd had a mostly female staff and had mostly printed poetry by female poets. I was the outsider who was supposed to freshen up the magazine and find new contributors, and the first thing I did was organize a contest to rename it. The red-haired former editor relinquished her post graciously, but without conceding that anything had been wrong with *The Nulset Review*. She was a languid, large-eyed woman with a soft, tremulous voice and a thirty-year-old Cuban boyfriend in New York. My staff and I spent the first half hour of our first edito-

*Take A Flying Fuck On A Rolling Doughnut.

rial meeting waiting for her to show up and tell us how to run a magazine. Finally, someone called her at home and woke her up—it was one o'clock on a Sunday afternoon—and she drifted in half an hour later, carrying an enormous mug of coffee and basically still sleeping. She lay on a sofa, her head pillowed in the nest of her curly red hair, and rarely spoke unless we were struggling to understand a submitted manuscript. Then, accepting the manuscript with a languid hand, she cast her eye over it briefly and delivered an incisive summary and analysis. I could see she was my competition. She was living upstairs from a grocery-and-meat market, in an off-campus apartment where the dark-haired French major I was chasing also lived. They were best friends. At a party in November, while everybody else was dancing, I found myself standing alone with the competition for the first time. I said, "I guess this means we finally have to have a conversation." She gave me a cold look, said, "No, it doesn't," and walked away.

I was making pretty good progress with the French major. One night in December she asked me to check the grammar in a paper on Alfred Döblin's *Berlin Alexanderplatz* which she was presenting in Avery's seminar the next day. I disagreed with her thesis in it, and at a certain point I realized that if I just kept discussing the book with her, we might end up spending the night together. We developed a better thesis—that Döblin's working-class hero, Franz Biberkopf, believes in masculine STRENGTH, but in order to find redemption he must admit his absolute weakness in the face of DEATH—and then, side by side, scribbling madly, smoking Marlboro Lights, we wrote a whole new paper. By the time we'd finished, at six in the morning, and were eating pancakes in an IHOP, I was so wired on nicotine and excited by the situation that I couldn't believe we wouldn't be falling straight into bed together after breakfast. But, my usual luck, she still had to type the paper.

On the last night of the semester, Ekström and I threw a big party. The French major was there, as were all our other friends and neighbors, and as were George and Doris Avery, who stayed for hours, sitting on Ekström's bed and drinking Gallo Hearty Burgundy and listening avidly to what our classmates had to say about literature and politics. I already suspected that Avery was the best teacher I would ever have, and I felt that he and Doris had done us a big favor by showing up and making our party extraordinary, not just a kid thing but a grownup thing as well; all evening, friends of mine came up to me and marveled, "They're such great people." I was aware, though, that I'd done the Averys a favor, too—that they didn't get invitations from students all that often. Every year an upperclassman or two fell under Avery's spell, but never more than one or two. And even though Avery was handsome and loyal and tenderhearted, he wasn't a lot more popular with his younger colleagues than he was with students. He had no patience with theory or political doctrine, and he was too obviously fascinated by good-looking women (just as Josef K. can't help mentioning to Fräulein Bürstner that a blouse of hers was hanging on her window, Avery was powerless, when speaking of certain female faculty, to omit descriptions of their clothes and bodies), and he was perhaps not always truthful in calling balls in or out on the tennis court, and he and his colleague Weber loathed each other so profoundly that they resorted to strange circumlocutions to avoid even pronouncing each other's names; and too often, when Avery was feeling insecure, he assaulted his and Doris's guests with hour-long recitations of raw literary-historical data, including, for example, the names and titles and capsule biographies of various contemporary archivists in Germany, Austria, and Switzerland. It was this other side of Avery—the fact that he so visibly *had* an other side—that was helping me finally understand all three of the dimensions in Kafka: that a man could

be a sweet, sympathetic, comically needy victim *and* a lascivi-
ous, self-aggrandizing, grudge-bearing bore, and also, crucially,
a third thing: a flickering consciousness, a simultaneity of cul-
pable urge and poignant self-reproach, a person in process.

Ekström and I had cleared the furniture from my bedroom
and made it the dance floor. Well past midnight, after the Averys and our less good friends had gone home, I found myself
alone on the floor, dancing to Elvis Costello's "(I Don't Want to
Go to) Chelsea" in my tightly wound way, while a group of people watched. *They were watching my expressivity*, I wrote in my
notebook the next day, on a plane to St. Louis. *I knew this, and
about a minute into the song I cast an "Oh so much attention show-
ered upon modest me" smile at the whole line of them. But I think my
real expressivity was in that smile. Why is he embarrassed? He's not
embarrassed, he loves attention. Well, he's embarrassed to get it, because he can't believe that other people can so quietly be party to his ex-
hibition. He's smiling with goodhearted disdain.* Then "Chelsea"
gave way to "Miss You," the Stones' moment in disco, and the
French major joined me on the floor. She said, "Now we're going to dance like we're freaked out!" The two of us brought our
faces close together, reached for each other, dodged each other,
and danced nose to nose in a freaked-out parody of attraction,
while people watched.

The house in Webster Groves looked tired. My parents were
suddenly old. I had the sense that Bob and his wife were secretly
appalled by them and planning a revolt. I couldn't understand
why Tom, who'd introduced me to the Talking Heads song
"Stay Hungry," which had been my personal anthem in Germany, kept talking about all the great food he'd been eating. My
father sat by the fireplace and read the story and the poem of
mine I'd printed in the literary magazine (new name: *Small*

Craft Warnings) and said to me, "Where is the story in these? Where are the word pictures? This is all ideas." My mother was a wreck. Twice, since September, she'd been in the hospital for knee operations, and now she was suffering with ulcerative colitis. Tom had brought home an unprecedentedly suitable new girlfriend in October, he'd given up filmmaking and was finding work as a building contractor, and the girlfriend seemed willing to overlook his lack of health insurance and conventional employment. But then my mother found out that the girlfriend wasn't suitable at all. She was, it turned out, cohabiting with Tom, and my mother could not be reconciled to this. It chewed away inside her. So did the imminence of my father's retirement, which she was dreading. She kept telling anyone who would listen that retirement was wrong for "able, vital people who can still contribute to society." Her phrasing was always the same.

For the first time in my life, I was starting to see the people in my family as actual people, not merely as relations, because I'd been reading German literature and was becoming a person myself. *Aber diesmal wird es geschrieben werden,** I wrote in my notebook on my first evening in St. Louis. I meant that this holiday with my family, unlike all the holidays in the past, would be recorded and analyzed in writing. I thought I was quoting from *Malte*. But Rilke's actual line is much crazier: *Aber diesmal werde ich geschrieben werden.*† Malte is envisioning a moment when, instead of being the maker of the writing ("I write"), he will be its product ("I am written"): instead of a performance, a transmission; instead of a focus on the self, a shining through the world. And yet I must not have been reading Rilke all that badly, because one of the family members I could now see more clearly

---

*But this time, it will be written.

†But this time, I will be written.

as a person was the youngest son, the warm puppy who amused the others with the cute things he said and then excused himself from the table and wrote cute sentences in his notebook; and I was running out of patience with this performer.

That night, after multiple dreams about the French major, each of which ended with her reproaching me for not wanting to have sex with her, I had a nightmare about the Averys' sweet-tempered German shepherd, Ina. In the dream, as I was sitting on the floor of the Averys' living room, the dog walked up to me and began to insult me. She said I was a frivolous, cynical, attention-seeking "fag" whose entire life had been phony. I answered her frivolously and cynically and chucked her under the chin. She grinned at me with malice, as if to make clear that she understood me to the core. Then she sank her teeth into my arm. As I fell over backward, she went for my throat.

I woke up and wrote: *So, eines morgens wurde er verhaftet.**

My mother took me aside and said viciously, regarding Tom's visit with his girlfriend in October, "They deceived me."

She looked up from a note she was writing at the dining-room table and asked me, "How do you spell 'emptiness'? Like, 'a feeling of emptiness'?"

All through Christmas dinner, she apologized for the absence of the traditional cranberry sorbet, which she'd been too tired to make this year. Each time she apologized, we assured her that we didn't miss the sorbet at all, the regular homemade cranberry sauce was all the cranberries any of us needed. A few minutes later, like a mechanical toy, she said she was sorry she hadn't made the traditional cranberry sorbet this year, but she was just too tired. After dinner, I went upstairs and took out my notebook, as I had many times before; but this time I was written.

*So, one morning he was arrested.

. . .

From a post-holiday letter of my mother's:

Dad feels your schedule is so light he's fearing he isn't getting his "money's worth" or something. Actually, sweetie, he is disappointed (perhaps I shouldn't tell you though I suspect you sense it) that you aren't graduating with a "saleable skill" as you promised—you've done what you loved, granted, but the real world is something else—& it has been *extremely* costly. I know, of course, you want to "write" but so do tens of thousands of other also talented young people & even I wonder how realistic you are at times. Well, keep us informed as to any encouraging or interesting developments—even a degree from Swarthmore is no guarantee of success, automatically. I hate being pessimistic (I've usually been a positive person) but I've seen how Tom has wasted his talents & I hope there won't be repetition.

From my letter in reply:

Perhaps I should make clear a few things that I had considered knowledge common to the three of us.

1. I am in the HONORS PROGRAM. In the honors program we take seminars that require large amounts of independent reading; each one is therefore considered the equivalent of two 4 or 5-hour courses . . .

2. Just when did I promise to graduate with what you continue to call a "saleable" major? What was this promise tied to? Your continued support of my education? All of this seems to have slipped my memory, you're right.

3. I know that by now you are reminding me weekly of how "*extremely* costly" Swarthmore is less for information's

sake than for rhetoric's. Yet I think you should know that there is a point where such repetition begins to have an effect directly opposite to the one you seek.

From my father's reply to my reply:

I feel that your letter needs a rebuttal as it contains so many critical—and some bitter—comments. It is a little difficult to reply without the letter from your mother but as background you should recognize by now that she is not always rational or tactful—and also consider that she has not felt well since last September . . . Even her knee is bothering again. She takes four different pills several times a day which I don't think is good for her. My analysis is that she has mental concerns that throw her out of balance physically. But I can't figure out what worries her. Her health is our only concern and that becomes a catch-22 situation.

And from my mother's reply to my reply:

How can I undo the damage I've done, hurting you as I did and feeling so down & so guilty ever since when, because of my love and respect for you (not only as my son but as one of the most special of all people in my life), I am depressed over the poor judgment & unreasonableness of the letter I wrote you when I was in an unfortunate mood. All I can say is, I'm sorry, I'm miserable over it, I trust you completely and I love you dearly — — — I beg your forgiveness and speak from my heart.

. . .

The last of the novels I'd read in German in the fall, and the one I'd resisted most staunchly, was *The Magic Mountain*. I'd resisted it because I understood it so much better than the other novels. Its young hero, Hans Castorp, is a bourgeois from the flatlands who goes for a three-week visit to a mountain sanatorium, gets sucked into the hermetic strangeness of the place, and ends up staying for seven years. Castorp is an innocent of the sort who might position himself at the Brain end of a Heart/Brain continuum, and Thomas Mann treats him with a loving irony and monstrous omniscience that together drove me crazy. Mann, as Avery helped us to see, has every symbol worked out perfectly: the bourgeois lowlands are the place of physical and moral health, the bohemian heights are the site of genius and disease, and what draws Castorp from the former up into the latter is the power of love—specifically, his attraction to his fellow patient Clawdia Chauchat. Clawdia really is the "hot cat" that her name in French denotes. She and Castorp exchange glances seven times in the sanatorium dining room, and he's staying in room 34 (3 + 4 = 7!) and she's in room 7, and their flirtation finally comes to a head on Walpurgis Night, exactly seven months after his arrival, when he approaches her on the pretext of borrowing a pencil, thereby repeating and fulfilling his bold borrowing of a pencil from a Clawdia-like boy he had a crush on long ago, a boy who warned him not to "break" the pencil, and he has sex with Clawdia once and only once, and never with anyone else, etc. etc. etc. And then, because so much formal perfection can be chilling, Mann throws in a tour de force chapter, "Snow," about the lethal chilliness of formal perfection, and proceeds to take the novel in a less hermetic direction, which is itself the formally perfect move to make.

The so-German organizational consciousness at work here made me groan the way an elaborate and successful pun does.

And yet at the heart of the book there was a question of genuine personal interest both to Mann and to me: How does it happen that a young person so quickly strays so far from the values and expectations of his middle-class upbringing? Superficially, in Castorp's case, you might think the fault lies with the little tubercular spot that shows up in his chest x-ray. But Castorp embraces his diagnosis so eagerly that you can see that it's more like a pretext—"ein abgekartetes Spiel."* The real reason he stays on at the sanatorium and watches his life become unrecognizable to him is that he's drawn to Clawdia's mons veneris, her so-called magic mountain. As Goethe put it, in his gendered language, "Das Ewig-Weibliche / Zieht uns hinan."† And part of what so annoyed me about Mann's ironic condescension to Castorp is its complicity in what seemed to me Castorp's passivity. He doesn't actively, restlessly abandon the bourgeois flatlands for an alpine bohemia; it's something that happens *to* him.

And happened to me, too. After the holidays, I went to Chicago and saw Tom, who was on his way to being a contractor and designer not unlike the one my father had imagined he should be, and I met his new girlfriend, Marta Smith, who was every bit as excellent as promised (and, indeed, less than a year later, became my mother's most trusted daughter-in-law). From Chicago, I returned to school a week early and stayed in the apartment above the meat market where the French major lived. Here it immediately became clear that the French major and I were sick of each other, sick of nothing happening. Her housemate, however, the red-haired New Yorker, my competition, had broken up with her Cuban boyfriend, and I sat and watched old movies with her after the rest of the house had gone to bed. She was the smartest person I'd ever met. She

*A card game in which the deck has been stacked.

†The Eternal-Feminine / Draws us upward.

could glance at a page of Wordsworth and tell you what Wordsworth was up to in every line. It turned out that she and I shared identical ambitions of putting childish things behind us, and that she, too, in her own way, was in flight from the flatlands. Before long, her voice was playing in my head around the clock. It occurred to me that my interest in her best friend, the French major, might never have been much more than an "abgekartetes Spiel." The competition and I went to dinner at the house of an off-campus student couple, mutual friends of ours, whose taste in food and clothes we afterward deplored in an orgy of like-mindedness. The following day, after the mail came, she asked me if I knew a person in Chicago named Marta Smith. This stranger Smith had somehow got her hands on a copy of *Small Craft Warnings*, read a long short story called "Dismembering You on Your Birthday," and spontaneously written to say she loved it. Marta knew nothing of my interest in the story's author, and the timing of her letter's arrival was like a mystical sign from a German novel of the sort I'd momentarily forgotten I didn't care for.

On the night of the competition's twenty-first (3 x 7th!) birthday, on January 24 (1/24 = 1+2+4 =7!), which was twenty-one (3 x 7!) days before Valentine's Day (14/2 = 7!)!, I came to her party with a pack of expensive Italian cigarettes as a present. The part of me that knew enough to fear enormous long-term complications was hoping that the two of us would just stay friends. But another, more important part of me must have felt otherwise (or so I later speculated, as Josef K. speculated that somebody "must have been" telling lies about him), because I was still on the couch with her at five the next morning, long after the party ended. When I apologized for keeping her up so late, the reply that issued from her infinitely soft, raw-cauliflower-tasting mouth was comforting and neat in the way that Mann was comforting and neat. "My idea of a perfect twenty-first birthday," she said, "certainly didn't include going to sleep before five."

One other scene from that sort of novel.

They'd been reading Freud intensively in the week before spring vacation. The little red-haired girl had a friend in the village center, a high-school teacher named Chloe, who had offered the girl and the boy the use of her apartment while she was on vacation. The girl and the boy were ready to do things in bed which were entirely new to the boy, if not to the girl, and which seemed to both of them too scream- ingly carnal for a mere hollow-core bedroom door to conceal from her housemates. So the two of them walked to Chloe's apartment on a Tuesday afternoon, during a break between spring showers. The mag- nolia petals they bruised underfoot were beaded with rain. In the girl's knapsack were bread, butter, eggs, gin, tonic water, coffee, cigarettes, and contraceptives. Chloe's apartment was a dark ground-floor unit in a featureless brick low-rise that the boy had passed a hundred times and never noticed. Its rooms were half empty following the departure of a boyfriend whom Chloe had badmouthed to the girl until she'd fi- nally found the courage to dump him. The girl and the boy made gin- and-tonics and went into Chloe's bedroom. Even though they'd locked the front door and nobody else was in the apartment, it was unthink- able not to shut Chloe's door behind them. To fall into bed in front of an open door was to invite a malevolent stranger to loom up in it while their attention was otherwise engaged; this happened in every teen horror movie ever made. The boy was still getting over his surprise that the girl wanted sex as much as he did, though why this had been such a surprise he could no longer say. He was just thankful for in- struction. Nothing this girl could do to him was dirty. The room itself, however, was plenty dirty. There was a musty carpet-pad smell and a big yellow stain on the ceiling. Clothes of Chloe's were hanging out of drawers, lying in a pile near the closet, hanging in a bulky mass from a hook on the hallway door. The girl was clean and fresh-smelling, but Chloe, whom the boy had never met, apparently was not. So it was dirty to be blown on Chloe's dirty bed. A rain shower pelted the room's only window furiously, behind a cheap and damaged plastic blind. The rain continued but was done before the boy and girl were. The sky was nearly dark when they got dressed and went out for a walk and cigarettes. In the west, a narrow panel of clear blue-green sky was visible between receding rain clouds and a warmly lighted college building. Even after cigarettes, the boy could taste the magic in his mouth. In his chest was a feeling of gratitude and embarrassment so large that he whimpered a little, involuntarily, every time his mind alit on what the girl had done for him and let him do.

It was night when they returned to Chloe's apartment and found that somebody had been inside it while they were gone. The front door, which they'd been careful to lock, was now unlocked. At the end of the hallway, in the kitchen, which they'd left dark, they could see a light burning brightly. "Hello?" the boy called. ". . . Hello? . . . Hello!" There was no answer. Nobody in the kitchen. The boy asked if Chloe's boyfriend might still have a house key. The girl, taking ice from the freezer for a gin-and-tonic, said it seemed unlikely, given that the guy had moved all his stuff out. "He also owes Chloe half a year of rent," the girl said, opening the refrigerator, and then: "Shit! SHIT! SHIT!" The boy said "What?" and the girl said, "He's been here! Somebody!" Because the bottle of tonic water, which the boy and the girl had left more than half full, was almost empty now. They looked at each other, wide-eyed, and peered down the dark hallway. The boy wished he'd turned a light on. "Hello?" he called. "Is someone here?" The girl was pulling open drawers, looking for knives. But Chloe didn't seem to have anything larger than a steak knife. The girl took one of them and gave the boy another, and together they moved down the hallway, calling "Hello? Hello?" The living room was OK. So was the little study. But when the boy came to the bedroom door and gave it a push, the man on the other side of it pushed back. The man had a gun, and the boy grabbed the doorknob with both hands and wrenched it toward him and braced his feet on either side of the door, pulling as hard as he could against significant resistance. For a moment, he heard the man with the gun huffing on the other side of the door. Then nothing. The boy kept pulling with all his strength. Both he and the girl were panting with terror. "What do I do?" she said. "Go, go, go, get out," he said hoarsely, "get outside!" She ran to the front door and opened it, looking back at the boy, who was still pulling on the doorknob. He was only eight steps away from her. He could be outside before the man with the gun got the door open and raised his weapon. And so the boy made his break. He and the girl flung themselves through the building's lobby and onto the sidewalk and stood there breathing hard. It was six in the evening in a pleasant suburb. Commuters coming home from work, somebody shooting baskets across the street, a winter chill reemerging from the shadows. As the boy and the girl stood on the sidewalk, shivering in the chill, they felt at once sheepish and extraordinary, as if nothing of this sort had ever happened—could ever happen—to anyone in the world but them. From feeling this to getting married would be no scarier a dash than from the bedroom door to safety. "I suppose it's fair to ask," the girl said, shivering, "why exactly Chloe's boyfriend would want to harm us." The boy, too, wondered if perhaps the weight and the sounds on the other side of the door had simply been Chloe's clothes, swinging on hangers. The world was becoming rational again. There would be a sticky pool of tonic water on the refrigerator's bottom shelf, something funky with the front-door lock, a timer on the kitchen light. The boy and the girl would go inside together and put the Unconscious in its place.

MY BIRD PROBLEM

South Texas: I'd checked into a roadside motel in Brownsville and was getting up in the dark every morning, making coffee for my old friend Manley, who wouldn't talk
to me or leave his bed until he'd had some, and then bolting the
motel's free breakfast and running to our rental car and birding
nonstop for twelve hours. I waited until nightfall to buy lunch
food and fill the car with gas, to avoid wasting even a minute of
birdable daylight. The only way not to question what I was doing, and why I was doing it, was to do absolutely nothing else.

At the Santa Ana National Wildlife Refuge, on a hot weekday afternoon, Manley and I hiked several miles down dusty
trails to an artificial water feature on the far margin of which I
saw three pale-brown ducks. Two of them were paddling with
all deliberate speed into the cover of dense reeds, affording me
a view mainly of their butts, but the third bird loitered long
enough for me to train my binoculars on its head, which looked
as if a person had dipped two fingers in black ink and drawn
horizontal lines across its face.

"A masked duck!" I said. "You see it?"

"I see the duck," Manley said.

"A masked duck!"

The bird quickly disappeared into the reeds and gave no sign of reemerging. I showed Manley its picture in my *Sibley*.

"I'm not familiar with this duck," he said. "But the bird in this picture is the one I just saw."

"The stripes on its face. The sort of cinnamony brown."

"Yes."

"It was a masked duck!"

We were within a few hundred yards of the Rio Grande. On the other side of the river, if you traveled south—say, to Brazil—you could see masked ducks by the dozens. They were a rarity north of the border, though. The pleasure of the sighting sweetened our long tramp back to the parking lot.

While Manley lay down in the car to take a nap, I poked around in a nearby marsh. Three middle-aged white guys with good equipment asked me if I'd seen anything interesting.

"Not much," I said, "except a masked duck."

All three began to talk at once.

"A masked duck!"

"Masked duck?"

"Where exactly? Show us on the map."

"Are you sure it was a masked duck?"

"You're familiar with the ruddy duck. You do know what a female ruddy looks like."

"Masked duck!"

I said that, yes, I'd seen female ruddies, we had them in Central Park, and this wasn't a ruddy duck. I said it was as if somebody had dipped two fingers in black ink and—

"Was it alone?"

"Were there others?"

"A masked duck!"

One of the men took out a pen, wrote down my name, and

had me pinpoint the location on a map. The other two were already moving down the trail I'd come up.

"And you're sure it was a masked duck," the third man said.

"It wasn't a ruddy," I said.

A fourth man stepped out of some bushes right behind us. "I've got a nighthawk sleeping in a tree."

"This guy saw a masked duck," the third man said.

"A masked duck! Are you sure? Are you familiar with the female ruddy?"

The other two men came hurrying back up the trail. "Did someone say nighthawk?"

"Yeah, I've got a scope on it."

The five of us went into the bushes. The nighthawk, asleep on a tree branch, looked like a partly balled gray hiking sock. The scope's owner said that the friend of his who'd first spotted the bird had called it a lesser nighthawk, not a common. The well-equipped trio begged to differ.

"He said lesser? Did he hear its call?"

"No," the man said. "But the range—"

"Range doesn't help you."

"Range argues for common, if anything, at this time of year."

"Look where the wing bar is."

"Common."

"Definitely calling it a common."

The four men set off at a forced-march pace to look for the masked duck, and I began to worry. My identification of the duck, which had felt ironclad in the moment, seemed dangerously hasty in the context of four serious birders marching several miles in the afternoon heat. I went and woke up Manley.

"The only thing that matters," he said, "is that we saw it."

"But the guy took my name down. Now, if they don't see it, I'm going to get a bad rep."

"If they don't see it, they'll think it's in the reeds."

"But what if they see ruddies instead? There could be ruddies *and* masked ducks, and the ruddies aren't as shy."

"It's something to be anxious about," Manley said, "if you want to be anxious about something."

I went to the refuge visitor center and wrote in the logbook: *One certain and two partially glimpsed* MASKED DUCKS, *north end of Cattail #2*. I asked a volunteer if anyone else had reported a masked duck.

"No, that would be our first this winter," she said.

The next afternoon, on South Padre Island, in the wetland behind the Convention Center, where about twenty upper-Midwestern retirees and scraggly-bearded white guys were pacing the boardwalks with cameras and binoculars, I saw a pretty, dark-haired young woman taking telephoto pictures of a pair of ducks. "Green-winged teals," I mentioned to Manley.

The girl looked up sharply. "Green-winged teals? Where?"

I nodded at her birds.

"Those are wigeons," she said.

"Right."

I'd made this mistake before. I knew perfectly well what a wigeon looked like, but sometimes, in the giddiness of spotting something, my brain got confused. As Manley and I retreated down the boardwalk, I showed him pictures.

"See," I said, "the wigeon and the green-winged teal have more or less the same palette, just completely rearranged. I should have said wigeon. Now she thinks I can't tell a wigeon from a teal."

"Why didn't you just tell her that?" Manley said. "Just say that the wrong word came out of your mouth."

"That would only have compounded it. It would have been protesting too much."

"But at least she'd know you know the difference."

"She doesn't know my name. I'll never see her again. That is my only conceivable consolation."

There is no better American place for birds in February than South Texas. Although Manley had been down here thirty years earlier, as a teenage birder, it was a wholly new world to me. In three days, I'd seen fetchingly disheveled anis flopping around on top of shrubs, Jurassic-looking anhingas sun-drying their wings, squadrons of white pelicans gliding downriver on nine-foot wingspans, a couple of caracaras eating a road-killed king snake, an elegant trogon and a crimson-collared grosbeak and two exotic robins all lurking on a postage-stamp Audubon Society tract in Weslaco. The only frustration was my No. 1 trip target bird, the black-bellied whistling-duck. A tree nester, strangely long-legged, with a candy-pink bill and a bold white eye ring, the whistling-duck was one of those birds in the field guide which I couldn't quite believe existed—something out of Marco Polo. It was supposed to winter in good numbers on Brownsville's urban oxbow lakes (called *resacas*), and with each shoreline that I scanned in vain, the bird became that much more mythical to me.

Out on South Padre, as fog rolled in off the Gulf of Mexico, I remembered to look up at the city water tower, where, according to my guidebook, a peregrine falcon often perched. Sure enough, very vaguely, I saw the peregrine up there. I set up my spotting scope, and an older couple, two seasoned-looking birders, asked me what I had.

"Peregrine falcon," I said proudly.

"You know, Jon," Manley said, his eye to the scope, "the head looks more like an osprey."

"That is an osprey," the woman quietly affirmed.

"*God*," I said, looking again, "it is *so hard* to tell in the fog, and to get a sense of scale, you know, way up there, but you're right, yes, I see it. Osprey, osprey, osprey. Yes."

"That's the great thing about fog," the woman remarked. "You can see whatever you want."

Just then the dark-haired young woman came by with her tripod and big camera.

"Osprey," I told her confidently. "By the way, you know, I'm still totally writhing about saying 'teal' when I meant 'gadwall.'"

She stared at me. "*Gadwall?*"

Back in the car, using Manley's phone to avoid betraying my own name via caller ID, I called the visitor center at Santa Ana and asked if "people" had been reporting any masked ducks on the refuge.

"Yes, somebody did report one yesterday. Down at Cattails."

"Just one person?" I asked.

"Yes. I wasn't here. But somebody did report a masked duck."

"Fantastic!" I said—as if, by sounding excited, I could lend after-the-fact credibility to my own report. "I'll come look for it!"

Halfway back to Brownsville, on one of the narrow dirt roads that Manley liked to direct me down, we stopped to admire a lushly green-girdled blue *resaca* with the setting sun behind us. The delta in winter was too beautiful to stay embarrassed in for long. I got out of the car, and there, silent, on the shadowed side of the water, floating nonchalantly, as if it were the most natural thing in the world—which is, after all, the way of magical creatures in enchanted places—was my black-bellied whistling-duck.

It felt weird to return to New York. After the excitements of South Texas, I was hollow and restless, like an addict in withdrawal. It was a chore to make myself comprehensible to friends; I couldn't keep my mind on my work. Every night, I lay down with bird books and read about other trips I could take, studied the field markings of species I hadn't seen, and then dreamed vividly of birds. When two kestrels, a male and a female, possibly driven out of Central Park by the artist Christo and his wife, Jeanne-Claude, began showing up on a chimney outside my kitchen window and bloodying their beaks on fresh-killed mice, their dislocation seemed to mirror my own.

One night in early March, I went to the Society for Ethical Culture to hear Al Gore speak on the subject of global warming. I was expecting to be amused by the speech's rhetorical badness—to roll my eyes at Gore's intoning of "fate" and "mankind," his flaunting of his wonk credentials, his scolding of American consumers. But Gore seemed to have rediscovered a sense of humor. His speech was fun to listen to, if unbelievably depressing. For more than an hour, with heavy graphical support, he presented compelling evidence of impending climate-driven cataclysms that will result in unimaginable amounts of upheaval and suffering around the globe, possibly within my own lifetime. I left the auditorium under a cloud of grief and worry of the sort I'd felt as a teenager reading about nuclear war.

Ordinarily, in New York, I keep a tight rein on my environmental consciousness, confining it, ideally, to the ten minutes per year when I write my guilt-assuaging checks to groups like the Sierra Club. But Gore's message was so disturbing that I was nearly back to my apartment before I could think of some reasons to discount it. Like: wasn't I already doing more than most Americans to combat global warming? I didn't own a car, I lived in an energy-efficient Manhattan apartment, I was good about recycling. Also: wasn't the weather that night *unusually cold* for early March? And hadn't Gore's maps of Manhattan in the future, the island half-submerged by rising sea levels, all shown that the corner of Lexington and Eighty-first Street, where I live, would stay high and dry in even the worst-case scenario? The Upper East Side has a definite topography. It seemed unlikely that seawater from Greenland's melting ice cap would advance any farther than the Citarella market on Third Avenue, six blocks to the south and east. Plus, my apartment was way up on the tenth floor.

When I went inside, no kids came running to meet me, and this absence of kids seemed to clinch it: I was better off spending my anxiety budget on viral pandemics and dirty bombs than on global warming. Even if I had had kids, it would have been hard work for me to care about the climatic well-being of their children's children. Not having kids freed me altogether. Not having kids was my last, best line of defense against the likes of Al Gore.

There was only one problem. Trying to fall asleep that night, mentally replaying Gore's computer images of a desertified North America, I couldn't find a way not to care about the billions of birds and thousands of avian species that were liable to be wiped out worldwide. Many of the Texan places that I'd visited in February had elevations of less than twenty feet, and the climate down there was already almost lethally extreme. Human beings could probably adapt to future changes, we were famously creative at averting disasters and at making up great stories when we couldn't, but birds didn't have our variety of options. Birds needed help. And this, I realized, was the true disaster for a comfortable modern American. This was the scenario I'd been at pains to avert for many years: not the world's falling apart in the future, but my feeling inconveniently obliged to care about it in the present. This was my bird problem.

For a long time, back in the eighties, my wife and I lived on our own little planet. We spent thrilling, superhuman amounts of time by ourselves. In our first two apartments, in Boston, we were so absorbed in each other that we got along with exactly one good friend, our college classmate Ekström, and when we finally moved to Queens, Ekström moved to Manhattan, thereby sparing us the need to find a different friend.

Early in our marriage, when my old German instructor Weber asked me what the two of us were doing for a social life, I said we didn't have one. "That's sweet for a year," Weber said. "Two years at the most." His certainty offended me. It struck me as extremely condescending, and I never spoke to him again.

None of the doom criers among our relatives and former friends, none of these brow-furrowing emotional climatologists, seemed to recognize the special resourcefulness of our union. To prove them wrong, we made our aloneness work for four years, for five years, for six years; and then, when the domestic atmosphere really did begin to overheat, we fled from New York to a Spanish village where we didn't know anybody and the villagers hardly even spoke Spanish. We were like those habit-bound peoples in Jared Diamond's *Collapse* who respond to an ecosystem's degradation by redoubling their demands on it—medieval Greenlanders, prehistoric Easter Islanders, contemporary SUV buyers. Whatever reserves the two of us still had when we arrived in Spain were burned up in seven months of isolation.

Returning to Queens, we could no longer stand to be together for more than a few weeks, couldn't stand to see each other so unhappy, without running somewhere else. We reacted to minor fights at breakfast by lying facedown on the floor of our respective rooms for hours at a time, waiting for acknowledgment of our pain. I wrote poisonous jeremiads to family members who I felt had slighted my wife; she presented me with handwritten fifteen- and twenty-page analyses of our condition; I was putting away a bottle of Maalox every week. It was clear to me that something was terribly wrong. And what was wrong, I decided, was modern industrialized society's assault on the environment.

In the early years, I'd been too poor to care about the environment. My first car in Massachusetts was a vinyl-top '72 Nova that needed a tailwind to achieve ten miles a gallon and whose exhaust was boeuf bourguignon–like in its richness and complexity. After the Nova died, we got a Malibu wagon whose ridiculous four-barrel carburetor ($800) needed replacing and whose catalytic converter ($350) had had its guts scraped out to ease the flow of gases. Polluting the air a little less would have cost us two or three months' living expenses. The Malibu practically knew its own way to the crooked garage where we bought our annual smog-inspection sticker.

The summer of 1988, however, had been one of the hottest on record in North America, and rural Spain had been a spectacle of unchecked development and garbage-strewn hillsides and diesel exhaust, and after the dismantlement of the Berlin Wall the prospect of nuclear annihilation (my longtime pet apocalypse) was receding somewhat, and the great thing about the rape of nature, as an alternative apocalypse, was the opportunity it gave me to blame myself. I had grown up listening to daily lectures on personal responsibility. My father was a saver of string and pencil stubs and a bequeather of fantastic Swedish Protestant prejudices. (He considered it unfair to drink a cocktail at home before going to a restaurant, because restaurants depended on liquor sales for profits.) To worry about the Kleenexes and paper towels I was wasting and the water I was letting run while I shaved and the sections of the Sunday *Times* I was throwing away unread and the pollutants I was helping to fill the sky with every time I took an airplane came naturally to me. I argued passionately with a friend who believed that fewer BTUs were lost in keeping a house at 68 degrees overnight than in raising the temperature to 68 in the morning. Every time I washed out a peanut-butter jar, I tried to calculate whether less petroleum might be used in manufacturing a new jar than in heating the dishwater and transporting the old jar to a recycling center.

My wife moved out in December 1990. A friend had invited her to come and live in Colorado Springs, and she was ready to escape the pollution of her living space by me. Like modern industrialized society, I continued to bring certain crucial material benefits to our household, but these benefits came at an ever greater psychic cost. By fleeing to the land of open skies, my wife hoped to restore her independent nature, which years of too-married life had compromised almost beyond recognition. She rented a pretty apartment on North Cascade Avenue and sent me excited letters about the mountain weather. She became fascinated with narratives of pioneer women—tough, oppressed, resourceful wives who buried dead infants, watched freak June blizzards kill their crops and livestock, and survived to write about it. She talked about lowering her resting pulse rate below thirty.

Back in New York, I didn't believe we'd really separated. It may have become impossible for us to live together, but my wife's sort of intelligence still seemed to me the best sort, her moral and aesthetic judgments still seemed to me the only ones that counted. The smell of her skin and the smell of her hair were restorative, irreplaceable, the best. Deploring other people—their lack of perfection—had always been our sport. I couldn't imagine never smelling her again.

The next summer, we went car-camping in the West. I was frankly envious of my wife's new Western life, and I also wanted to immerse myself in nature, now that I'd become environmentally conscious. For a month, the two of us followed the retreating snow up through the Rockies and Cascades, and made our way back south through the emptiest country we could find. Considering that we were back together 24/7, sharing a small tent, and isolated from all social contacts, we got along remarkably well.

What sickened and enraged me were all the other human beings on the planet. The fresh air, the smell of firs, the torrents of snowmelt, the columbines and lupine, the glimpses of slender-ankled moose were nice sensations, but not intrinsically any nicer than a gin martini or a well-aged steak. To really deliver the goods, the West also had to conform to my wish that it be unpopulated and pristine. Driving down an empty road through empty hills was a way of reconnecting with childhood fantasies of being a Special Adventurer—of feeling again like the children in Narnia, like the heroes of Middle-earth. But house-sized tree pullers weren't clear-cutting Narnia behind a scrim of beauty strips. Frodo Baggins and his compatriots never had to share campgrounds with forty-five identical Fellowships of the Ring wearing Gore-Tex parkas from REI. Every crest in the open road opened up new vistas of irrigation-intensive monoculture, mining-scarred hillsides, and parking lots full of nature lovers' cars. To escape the crowds, my wife and I took longer hikes in deeper backcountry, toiling through switchbacks, only to find ourselves on dusty logging roads littered with horse manure. And here—look out!—came some gonzo clown on his mountain bike. And there, overhead, went Delta Flight 922 to Cincinnati. And here came a dozen Boy Scouts with jangling water cups and refrigerator-sized backpacks. My wife had her cardiovascular ambitions to occupy her, but I was free to stew all day long: Were those human voices up ahead?

Was that a speck of aluminum foil in the tree litter? Or, oh no, were those human voices coming up *behind us*?

I stayed in Colorado for a few more months, but being in the mountains had become unbearable to me. Why stick around to see the last beautiful wild places getting ruined, and to hate my own species, and to feel that I, too, in my small way, was one of the guilty ruiners? In the fall I moved back East. Eastern ecologies, specifically Philadelphia's, had the virtue of already being ruined. It eased my polluter's conscience to lie, so to speak, in a bed I'd helped to make. And this bed wasn't even so bad. For all the insults it had absorbed, the land in Pennsylvania was still riotously green.

The same could not be said of our marital planet. There, the time had come for me to take decisive action; the longer I delayed, the more damage I would do. Our once limitless-seeming supply of years for having kids, for example, had suddenly and alarmingly dwindled, and to dither for even just a few more years would be permanently ruinous. And yet: what decisive action to take? At this late date, I seemed to have only two choices. Either I should try to change myself radically—devote myself to making my wife happy, try to occupy less space, and be, if necessary, a full-time dad—or else I should divorce her.

Radically changing myself, however, was about as appetizing (and likely to happen) as volunteering for the drab, homespun, post-consumerist society that the "deep ecologists" tell us is the only long-term hope for humans on the planet. Although I talked the talk of fixing and healing, and sometimes I believed it, a self-interested part of me had long been rooting for trouble and waiting, with calm assurance, for the final calamity to engulf us. I had old journals containing transcripts of early fights which read word-for-word like the fights we were having ten years later. I had a carbon copy of a letter I'd written to my brother Tom in 1982, after I'd announced our engagement to my family and Tom had asked me why the two of us didn't just live together and see how things went; I'd replied that, in the Hegelian system, a subjective phenomenon (e.g., romantic love) did not become, properly speaking, "real" until it took its place in an objective structure, and that it was therefore important that the individual and the civic be synthesized in a ceremony of commitment. I had wedding pictures in which, before the ceremony of commitment, my wife looked beatific and I could be seen frowning and biting my lip and hugging myself tightly.

But giving up on the marriage was no less unthinkable. It was possible that we were unhappy because we were trapped in a bad relationship, but it was also possible that we were unhappy for other reasons, and that we should be patient and try to help each other. For every doubt documented in the fossil record, I could find an old letter or journal entry in which I talked about our marriage with happy certainty, as if we'd been together since the formation of the solar system, as if there had always been the two of us and always would be. The skinny, tuxedoed kid in our wedding pictures, once the ceremony was over, looked unmistakably smitten with his bride.

So more study was needed. The fossil record was ambiguous. The liberal scientific consensus was self-serving. Maybe, if we tried a new city, we could be happy? We traveled to check out San Francisco, Oakland, Portland, Santa Fe, Seattle, Boulder, Chicago, Utica, Albany, Syracuse, and Kingston, New York, finding things to fault in each of them. My wife came back and joined me in Philadelphia, and I borrowed money at interest from my mother and rented a three-story, five-bedroom house that neither of us could stand to live in by the middle of 1993. I sublet a place for myself in Manhattan which I then, out of guilt, handed over to my wife. I returned to Philadelphia and rented yet a third space, this one suitable for both working and sleeping, so that my wife would have all five of the house's bedrooms at her disposal, should she need them, on her return to Philly. Our financial hemorrhaging in late 1993 looked a lot like the country's energy policy in 2005. Our determination to cling to unsustainable dreams was congruent with—maybe even identical to—our drive to bankrupt ourselves as rapidly as possible.

Around Christmastime, the money ran out altogether. We broke our leases and sold the furniture. I took the old car, she took the new laptop, I slept with other people. Unthinkable and horrible and ardently wished-for: our little planet was ruined.

A staple of my family's dinner-table conversation in the midseventies was the divorce and remarriage of my father's boss at the railroad, Mr. German. Nobody of my parents' generation in either of their extended families had ever been divorced, nor had any of their friends, and so the two of them steeled each other in their resolve not to know Mr. German's young second wife. They exhaustively pitied the first wife, "poor Glorianna," who had been so dependent on her husband that she'd never even learned to drive. They expressed relief and worry at the Germans' departure from their Saturday-night bridge club, since Mr. German was bad at bridge but Glorianna was now left without a social life. One night my father came home and said he'd almost lost his job that day at lunch. In the executive dining room, while Mr. German and his subordinates were discussing how to assess a person's character, my father had found himself remarking that he judged a man by how he played a bridge hand. I wasn't old enough to understand that he hadn't really almost lost his job for this, or that condemning Mr. German and pitying Glorianna were ways for my parents to talk about their own marriage, but I did understand that dumping your wife for a younger woman was the sort of despicable selfish thing that a chronic overbidder might do.

A related talk staple in those years was my father's hatred of the Environmental Protection Agency. The young agency had issued complicated rules about soil pollution and toxic runoff and riverbank erosion, and some of the rules seemed unreasonable to my father. What really enraged him, though, were the enforcers. Night after night he came home fuming about these "bureaucrats" and "academics," these high-handed "so-and-sos" who didn't bother to hide how morally and intellectually superior they felt to the corporations they were monitoring, and who didn't think they owed explanations, or even basic courtesy, to people like my father.

The odd thing was how closely my father's values resembled those of his enemies. The breakthrough environmental legislation of that era, including the Clean Air and Clean Water Acts and the Endangered Species Act, had attracted the support of President Nixon and both parties in Congress precisely because it made sense to old-fashioned Protestants, like my parents, who abhorred waste and made sacrifices for their kids' future and respected God's works and believed in taking responsibility for their messes. But the social ferment that gave rise to the first Earth Day, in 1970, unleashed a host of other energies—the incivility of the so-and-sos, the pleasurable self-realizations of Mr. German, the cult of individuality—that were inimical to the old religion and ultimately won out.

Certainly I, as a self-realizing individual in the nineties, was having trouble with my parents' logic of unselfishness. Deprive myself of an available pleasure *why?* Take shorter and colder showers *why?* Keep having anguished phone conversations with my estranged wife on the subject of our failure to have children *why?* Struggle to read Henry James's last three novels *why?* Stay mindful of the Amazon rain forest *why?* New York City, which I returned to for good in 1994, was becoming a very pleasant place to live again. The nearby Catskills and Adirondacks were better protected than the Rockies and Cascades. Central Park, under recultivation by deep-pocketed locals, was looking greener every spring, and the other people out walking in it didn't enrage me: this was a *city*; there were *supposed* to be other people. On a May night in 1996, I walked across the park's newly restored, deep-pile lawns to a party where I saw a beautiful and very young woman standing awkwardly in a corner, behind a floor lamp that she twice nearly knocked over, and I felt so liberated that I could no longer remember one single reason not to introduce myself to her and, in due course, start asking her out.

The old religion was finished. Without its cultural support, the environmental movement's own cult of wilderness was never going to galvanize mass audiences. John Muir, writing from San Francisco at a time when you could travel to Yosemite without hardship and still have the valley to yourself for spiritual refreshment, founded a religion that required a large parcel of empty backcountry for every worshipper. Even in 1880, there weren't enough parcels like this to go around. Indeed, for the next eighty years, until Rachel Carson and David Brower sounded their populist alarms, the preserving of wild nature was generally assumed to be the province of elites. The organization that Muir formed to defend his beloved Sierras was a Club, not an Alliance. Henry David Thoreau, whose feelings for pine trees were romantic, if not downright sexual, called the workers who felled them "vermin." For Edward Abbey, who was the rare green writer with the courage of his misanthropy, the appeal of southeastern Utah was, frankly, that its desert was inhospitable to the great herd of Americans who were incapable of understanding and respecting the natural world. Bill McKibben,

Harvard graduate, followed up his apocalyptic *The End of Nature* (in which he contrasted his own deep reverence for nature with the shallow-minded "hobby" that nature is for most outdoorspeople) with a book about cable TV's inferiority to the timeless pleasures of country living. To Verlyn Klinkenborg, the professional trivialist whose job is to remind *New York Times* readers that spring follows winter and summer follows spring, and who sincerely loves snowdrifts and baling twine, the rest of humanity is a distant blob notable for its "venality" and "ignorance."

And so, once the EPA had cleaned up the country's most glaring messes, once sea otters and peregrine falcons had rebounded from near extinction, once Americans had had a disagreeable taste of European-style regulation, the environmental movement began to look like just another special interest hiding in the skirts of the Democratic Party. It consisted of well-heeled nature enthusiasts, tree-spiking misanthropes, nerdy defenders of unfashionable values (thrift, foresight), invokers of politically unfungible abstractions (the welfare of our great-grandchildren), issuers of shrill warnings about invisible risks (global warming) and exaggerated hazards (asbestos in public buildings), tiresome scolds about consumerism, reliers on facts and policies in an age of image, a constituency loudly proud of its refusal to compromise with others. Bill Clinton, the first boomer President, knew a stinker when he saw one. Unlike Richard Nixon, who had created the EPA, and unlike Jimmy Carter, who had set aside twenty-five million acres of Alaska as permanent wilderness, Clinton needed the Sierra Club a lot less than it needed him. In the Pacific Northwest, on lands belonging to the American people, the U.S. Forest Service was spending millions of tax dollars to build roads for multinational timber companies that were clear-cutting gorgeous primeval forests and taking handsome profits for themselves, preserving a handful of jobs for loggers who would soon be out of work anyway, and shipping much of the timber to Asia for processing and sale. You wouldn't think this issue was an automatic public-relations loser, but groups like the Sierra Club decided to fight the battle out of public sight, in federal court, where their victories tended to be Pyrrhic; and the boomer President, whose need for love was nonsatiable by Douglas firs or spotted owls but conceivably could be met by lumberjacks, soon added the decimation of the Northwest's old-growth forests to a long list of related setbacks—an environmentally toothless NAFTA, the metastasis of exurban sprawl, the lowering of average national vehicle fuel efficiency, the triumph of the SUV, the accelerating depletion of the world's fisheries, the Senate's 95–0 demurral on the Kyoto Protocol, etc.—in the decade when I left my wife and took up with a twenty-seven-year-old and really started having fun.

Then my mother died, and I went out birdwatching for the first time in my life. This was in the summer of 1999. I was on Hat Island, a wooded loaf of gravel subdivided for small weekend homes, near the blue-collar town of Everett, Washington. There were eagles and kingfishers and Bonaparte's gulls and dozens of identical sparrows that persisted, no matter how many times I studied them, in resembling six different sparrow species in the field guide I was using. Flocks of goldfinches brilliantly exploded up over the island's sunlit bluffs like something ceremonial and Japanese. I saw my first northern flicker and enjoyed its apparent confusion about what kind of bird it was. Unwoodpeckerish in plumage, like a mourning dove in war paint, it flew dippingly, in typical woodpecker fashion, white rump flashing, from one ill-fitting identity to another. It had a way of landing with a little crash wherever. In its careening beauty it reminded me of my former girlfriend, the one I'd first glimpsed tangling with a floor lamp and was still very fond of, though from a safe remove now.

I had since met a vegetarian Californian writer, a self-described "fool for animals," slightly older than I, who had no discernible interest in getting pregnant or married or in moving to New York. As soon as I'd fallen for her, I'd set about trying to change her personality and make it more like mine; and although, a year later, I had nothing to show for this effort, I at least didn't have to worry about ruining somebody again. The Californian was a veteran of a ruinous marriage of her own. Her indifference to the idea of kids spared me from checking my watch every five minutes to see if it was time for my decision about her reproductive future. The person who wanted kids was me. And, being a man, I could afford to take my time.

The last day I ever spent with my mother, at my brother's house in Seattle, she asked me the same questions over and over: Was I pretty sure that the Californian was the woman I would end up with? Did I think we would probably get married? Was the Californian actually divorced yet? Was she interested in having a baby? Was I? My mother was hoping for a glimpse of how my life might proceed after she was gone. She'd met the Californian only once, at a noisy restaurant in Los Angeles, but she wanted to feel that our story would continue and that she'd participated in it in some small way, if only by expressing her opinion that the Californian really ought to be divorced by now. My mother loved to be a part of things, and having strong opinions was a way of not feeling left out. At any given moment in the last twenty years of her life, family members in three time zones could be found worrying about her strong opinions or loudly declaring that they didn't care about them or phoning each other for advice on how to cope with them.

Whoever imagined that LOVE YOUR MOTHER would make a good environmental bumper sticker obviously didn't have a mom like mine. Well into the nineties, tailing Subarus or Volvos outfitted with this admonition and its accompanying snapshot of Earth, I felt obscurely hectored by it, as if the message were "Nature Wonders Why She Hasn't Heard from You in Nearly a Month" or "Our Planet *Strongly* Disapproves of Your Lifestyle" or "The Earth Hates to Nag, But . . ." Like the natural world, my mother had not been in the best of health by the time I was born. She was thirty-eight, she'd had three successive miscarriages, and she'd been suffering from ulcerative colitis for a decade. She kept me out of nursery school because she didn't want to let go of me for even a few hours a week. She sobbed frighteningly when my brothers went off to college. Once they were gone, I faced nine years of being the last handy object of her maternal longings and frustrations and criticisms, and so I allied myself with my father, who was embarrassed by her emotion. I began by rolling my eyes at everything she said. Over the next twenty-five years, as she went on to have acute phlebitis, a pulmonary embolism, two knee replacements, a broken femur, three miscellaneous orthopedic surgeries, Raynaud's disease, arthritis, biannual colonoscopies, monthly blood-clot tests, extreme steroidal facial swelling, congestive heart failure, and glaucoma, I often felt terribly sorry for her, and I tried to say the right things and be a dutiful son, but it wasn't until she got a bad cancer diagnosis, in 1996, that I began to do what those bumper stickers admonished me to do.

She died in Seattle on a Friday morning. The Californian, who had been due to arrive that evening and spend some days getting acquainted with her, ended up alone with me for a week at my brother's vacation house on Hat Island. I broke down in tears every few hours, which I took as a sign that I was working through my grief and would soon be over it. I sat on the lawn with binoculars and watched a spotted towhee scratch vigorously in the underbrush, like somebody who really enjoyed yard work. I was pleased to see chestnut-backed chickadees hopping around in conifers, since, according to the guidebook, conifers were their favored habitat. I kept a list of the species I'd seen.

By midweek, though, I'd found a more compelling pastime: I began to badger the Californian about having children and the fact that she wasn't actually divorced yet. In the style of my mother, who had been a gifted abrader of the sensitivities of people she was unhappy with, I gathered and collated all the faults and weaknesses that the Californian had ever privately confessed to me, and I showed her how these interrelated faults and weaknesses were preventing her from deciding, *right now*, whether we would probably get married and whether she wanted to have children. By the end of the week, fully seven days after my mother's death, I was sure I was over the worst of my grief, and so I was mystified and angered by the Californian's unwillingness to move to New York and immediately try to get pregnant. Even more mystified and angered a month later, when she took wing to Santa Cruz and refused to fly back.

On my first visit to the cabin where she lived, in the Santa Cruz Mountains, I'd stood and watched mallards swimming in the San Lorenzo River. I was struck by how frequently a male and a female paired up, one waiting on the other while it nosed in the weeds. I had no intention of living without steak or bacon, but after that trip, as a token of vegetarianism, I decided to stop eating duck. I asked my friends what they knew about ducks. All agreed that they were beautiful animals; several also commented that they did not make good pets.

In New York, while the Californian took refuge from me in her cabin, I seethed with strong opinions. *The only thing I wanted* was for her and me to be in the same place, and I would gladly have gone out to California *if only she'd told me up front* that she wasn't coming back to New York. The more months that went by without our getting closer to a pregnancy, the more aggressively I argued for living together, and the more aggressively I argued, the flightier the Californian became, until I felt I had no choice but to issue an ultimatum, which resulted in a breakup, and then a more final ultimatum, which resulted in a more final breakup, and then a final final ultimatum, which resulted in a final final breakup, shortly after which I went out walking along the lake in lower Central Park and saw a male and a female mallard swimming side by side, nosing in the weeds together, and burst into tears.

It wasn't until a year or more later, after the Californian had changed her mind and come to New York, that I faced medical facts and admitted to myself that we weren't just going to up and have a baby. And even then I thought: Our domestic life is good right now, but if I ever feel like trying a different life with somebody else, I'll have a ready-made escape route from my current one: "Didn't I always say I wanted children?" Only after I turned forty-four, which was my father's age when I was born, did I get around to wondering why, if I was so keen to have kids, I'd chosen to pursue a woman whose indifference to the prospect had been clear from the beginning. Was it possible that I only wanted kids with this one particular person, because I loved her? It was apparent, in any case, that my wish for kids had become nontransferable. I was not Henry the Eighth. It wasn't as if I found fertility a lovable personality trait or a promising foundation for a lifetime of great conversation. On the contrary, I seemed to meet a lot of very boring fertile people.

Finally, sadly, around Christmastime, I came to the conclusion that my ready-made escape route had disappeared. I might find some other route later, but this route was no more. For a while, in the Californian's cabin, I was able to take seasonal comfort in stupefying amounts of aquavit, champagne, and vodka. But then it was New Year's, and I faced the question of what to do with myself for the next thirty childless years; and the next morning I got up early and went looking for the Eurasian wigeon that had been reported in south Santa Cruz County.

My affair with birds had begun innocently—an encounter on Hat Island, a morning of sharing binoculars with friends on Cape Cod. I wasn't properly introduced until a warm spring Saturday when the Californian's sister and brother-in-law, two serious birders who were visiting New York for spring migration, took me walking in Central Park. We started at Belvedere Castle, and right there, on mulchy ground behind the weather station, we saw a bird shaped like a robin but light-breasted and feathered in russet tones. A veery, the brother-in-law said.

I'd never even heard of veeries. The only birds I'd noticed on my hundreds of walks in the park were pigeons and mallards and, from a distance, beyond a battery of telescopes, the nesting red-tailed hawks that had become such overexposed celebrities. It was weird to see a foreign, unfamous veery hopping around in plain sight, five feet away from a busy footpath, on a day when half of Manhattan was sunning in the park. I felt as if, all my life, I'd been mistaken about something important. I followed my visitors into the Ramble in agreeably engrossed disbelief, as in a dream in which yellowthroats and redstarts and black-throated blue and black-throated green warblers had been placed like ornaments in urban foliage, and a film production unit had left behind tanagers and buntings like rolls of gaffer's tape, and ovenbirds were jogging down the Ramble's eroded hillsides like tiny costumed stragglers from some Fifth Avenue parade: as if these birds were just momentary bright litter, and the park would soon be cleaned up and made recognizable again.

Which it was. By June, the migration was over; songbirds were no longer flying all night and arriving in New York at dawn, seeing bleak expanses of pavement and window, and heading to the park for refreshment. But that Saturday afternoon had taught me to pay more attention. I started budgeting extra minutes when I had to cross the park to get somewhere. Out in the country, from the windows of generic motels, I looked at the cattails and sumac by interstate overpasses and wished I'd brought binoculars. A glimpse of dense brush or a rocky shoreline gave me an infatuated feeling, a sense of the world's being full of possibility. There were new birds to look for everywhere, and little by little I figured out the best hours (morning) and the best places (near some water) to go looking. Even then, it sometimes happened that I would walk through the park and see no bird more unusual than a starling, literally not one, and I would feel unloved and abandoned and wronged. (The stupid birds: where were they?) But then, later in the week, I'd see a spotted sandpiper by the Turtle Pond, or a hooded merganser on the Reservoir, or a green heron in some dirt by the Bow Bridge, and be happy.

Birds were what became of dinosaurs. Those mountains of flesh whose petrified bones were on display at the Museum of Natural History had done some brilliant retooling over the ages and could now be found living in the form of orioles in the sycamores across the street. As solutions to the problem of earthly existence, the dinosaurs had been pretty great, but blue-headed vireos and yellow warblers and white-throated sparrows—feather-light, hollow-boned, full of song—were even greater. Birds were like dinosaurs' better selves. They had short lives and long summers. We all should be so lucky as to leave behind such heirs.

The more I looked at birds, the more I regretted not making their acquaintance sooner. It seemed to me a sadness and a waste that I'd spent so many months out West, camping and hiking amid ptarmigans and solitaires and other fantastic birds, and had managed, in all that time, to notice and remember only one: a long-billed curlew in Montana. How different my marriage might have been if I'd been able to go birding! How much more tolerable our year in Spain might have been made by European waterfowl!

And how odd, come to think of it, that I'd grown up unscathed by Phoebe Snetsinger, the mom of one of my Webster Groves classmates, who later became the most successful birder in the world. After she was diagnosed with metastatic malignant melanoma, in 1981, Snetsinger decided to devote the remaining months of her life to really serious birding, and over the next two decades, through repeated remissions and recurrences, she saw more species than any other human being before or since; her list was near eighty-five hundred when she was killed in a road accident while chasing rarities in Madagascar. Back in the seventies, my friend Manley had come under Snetsinger's influence. He finished high school with a life list of better than three hundred species, and I was more interested in science than Manley was, and yet I never aimed my binoculars at anything but the night sky.

One reason I didn't was that the best birders at my high school were serious potheads and acid users. Also, most of them were boys. Birding wasn't necessarily nerdy (nerds didn't come to school tripping), but the scene associated with it was not my idea of galvanic. Of romantic. Tramping in woods and fields for ten hours, steadily looking at birds, not communicating about anything but birds, spending a Saturday that way, was strikingly akin, as a social experience, to getting baked.

Which itself may have been one reason why, in the year following my introduction to the veery, as I began to bird more often and stay out longer, I had a creeping sense of shame about what I was doing. Even as I was learning my gulls and sparrows, I took care, in New York, not to wear my binoculars on a strap but to carry them cupped discreetly in one hand, and if I brought a field guide to the park, I made sure to keep the front cover, which had the word BIRDS in large type, facing inward. On a trip to London, I mentioned to a friend there, a book editor who is a very stylish dresser, that I'd seen a green woodpecker eating ants in Hyde Park, and he made a horrible face and said, "Oh, Christ, don't tell me you're a twitcher." An American friend, the editor of a design magazine, also a sharp dresser, similarly clutched her head when I told her I'd been looking at birds. "No, no, no, no, no, no," she said. "You are *not* going to be a birdwatcher."

"Why not?"

"Because birdwatchers—*ucch*. They're all so—*ucch*."

"But if *I'm* doing it," I said, "and if I'm not that way—"

"But that's the thing!" she said. "You're going to *become* that way. And then I won't want to see you anymore."

She was talking in part about accessories, such as the elastic harness that birders attach to their binoculars to minimize neck strain and whose nickname, I'm afraid, is "the bra." But the really disturbing specter that my friend had in mind was the un-defended sincerity of birders. The nakedness of their seeking. Their so-public twitching hunger. The problem was less acute in the shady Ramble (whose recesses, significantly, are popular for both daytime birding and nighttime gay cruising); but in highly public New York places, like on the Bow Bridge, I couldn't bear to hold my binoculars to my eyes for more than a few seconds. It was just too embarrassing to feel, or to imagine, that my private transports were being witnessed by better-defended New Yorkers.

And so it was in California that the affair really took off. My furtive hour-long get-togethers gave way to daylong escapes that I openly spent birding, wearing the bra. I set the alarm clock in the Californian's cabin for gruesomely early hours. To be juggling a stick shift and a thermos of coffee when the roads were still gray and empty, to be out ahead of everyone, to see no headlights on the Pacific Coast Highway, to be the only car pulled over at Rancho del Oso State Park, to already be on site when the birds were waking up, to hear their voices in the willow thickets and the salt marsh and the meadow whose scattered oaks were draped with epiphytes, to sense the birds' collective beauty imminent and findable in there: what a pure joy this all was. In New York, when I hadn't slept enough, my face ached all day; in California, after my first morning look at a foraging grosbeak or a diving scoter, I felt connected to a nicely calibrated drip of speed. Days passed like hours. I moved at the same pace as the sun in the sky; I could almost feel the earth turning. I took a short, hard nap in my car and woke up to see two golden eagles arrogantly working a hillside. I stopped at a feed lot to look for tricolored and yellow-headed blackbirds amid a thousand more plebeian birds, and what I saw instead, when the multitude wheeled into defensive flight, was a merlin coming to perch on a water tower. I walked for a mile in promising woods and saw basically nothing, a retreating thrush, some plain-Jane kinglets, and then, just as I was remembering what a monumental waste of time birding was, the woods came alive with songbirds, something fresh on every branch, and for the next fifteen minutes each birdlike movement in the woods was a gift to be unwrapped—western wood-pewee, MacGillivray's warbler, pygmy nuthatch—and then, just as suddenly, the wave was gone again, like inspiration or ecstasy, and the woods were quiet.

Always, in the past, I'd felt like a failure at the task of being satisfied by nature's beauty. Hiking in the West, my wife and I had sometimes found our way to summits unruined by other hikers, but even then, when the hike was perfect, I would wonder, "Now what?" And take a picture. Take another picture. Like a man with a photogenic girlfriend he didn't love. As if, unable to be satisfied myself, I at least might impress somebody else later on. And when the picture-taking finally came to feel just too pointless, I took mental pictures. I enlisted my wife to agree that such-and-such vista was incredible, I imagined myself in a movie with this vista in the background and various girls I'd known in high school and college watching the movie and being impressed with me; but nothing worked. The stimulations remained stubbornly theoretical, like sex on Prozac.

Only now, when nature had become the place where birds were, did I finally get what all the fuss was about. The California towhee that I watched at breakfast every morning, the plainest of medium-small brown birds, a modest ground dweller, a giver of cheerful, elementary chipping calls, brought me more pleasure than Half Dome at sunrise or the ocean shoreline at Big Sur. The California towhee generally, the whole species, reliably uniform in its plumage and habits, was like a friend whose energy and optimism had escaped the confines of a single body to animate roadsides and back yards across thousands of square miles. And there were 650 other species that bred in the United States and Canada, a population so varied in look and habitat and behavior—cranes, hummingbirds, eagles, shearwaters, snipe—that, taken as a whole, they were like a companion with an inexhaustibly rich personality. They made me happy like nothing outdoors ever had.

My response to this happiness, naturally, was to worry that I was in the grip of something diseased and bad and wrong. An addiction. Every morning, driving to an office I'd borrowed in Santa Cruz, I would wrestle with the urge to stop and bird for "a few minutes." Seeing a good bird made me want to stay out and see more good birds. Not seeing a good bird made me sour and desolate, for which the only cure was, likewise, to keep looking. If I did manage not to stop for "a few minutes," and if my work then didn't go well, I would sit and think about how high the sun was getting and how stupid I'd been to chain myself to my desk. Finally, toward noon, I would grab my binoculars, at which point the only way not to feel guilty about blowing off a workday was to focus utterly on the rendezvous, to open a field guide against the steering wheel and compare, for the twentieth time, the bill shapes and plumages of Pacific and red-throated loons. If I got stuck behind a slow car or made a wrong turn, I swore viciously and jerked the wheel and crushed the brakes and floored the accelerator.

I worried about my problem, but I couldn't stop. On business trips, I took whole personal days for birding, in Arizona and Minnesota and Florida, and it was here, on these solitary trips, that my affair with birds began to compound the very grief I was seeking refuge from. Phoebe Snetsinger, in her pointedly titled memoir, *Birding on Borrowed Time*, had described how many of the great avian haunts she'd visited in the eighties were diminished or destroyed by the late nineties. Driving on new arteries, seeing valley after valley sprawled over, habitat after habitat wiped out, I became increasingly distressed about the plight of wild birds. The ground dwellers were being killed by the tens of millions by domestic and feral cats, the low fliers were getting run down on ever-expanding exurban roads, the medium fliers were dismembering themselves on cellphone towers and wind turbines, the high fliers were colliding with brightly lit skyscrapers or mistaking rain-slick parking lots for lakes or landing in "refuges" where men in boots lined up to shoot them. On Arizona roads, the least fuel-efficient vehicles identified themselves with American flags and bumper-sticker messages like IF YOU CAN'T FEED 'EM, DON'T BREED 'EM. The Bush Administration claimed that Congress never intended the Endangered Species Act to interfere with commerce if local jobs were at stake—in effect, that endangered species should enjoy federal protection only on land that nobody had any conceivable commercial use for. The country as a whole had become so hostile to the have-nots that large numbers of the have-nots themselves now voted against their own economic interests.

The difficulty for birds, in a political climate like this, is that they are just profoundly poor. To put it as strongly as possible: they subsist on bugs. Also on worms, seeds, weeds, buds, rodents, minnows, pond greens, grubs, and garbage. A few lucky species—what birders call "trash birds"—cadge a living in urban neighborhoods, but to find more interesting species it's best to go to sketchy areas: sewage ponds, landfills, foul-smelling mudflats, railroad rights-of-way, abandoned buildings, tamarack swamps, thornbushes, tundra, weedy slashes, slime-covered rocks in shallow lagoons, open plains of harsh sawgrass, manure pits on dairy farms, ankle-turning desert washes. The species that reside in and around these bird ghettos are themselves fairly lucky. It's the birds with more expensive tastes, the terns and plovers that insist on beachfront housing, the murrelets and owls that nest in old-growth forests, that end up on endangered-species lists.

Birds not only want to use our valuable land, they're also hopelessly unable to pay for it. In Minnesota, north of Duluth, on an overcast morning when the temperature was hovering near ten, I saw a clan of white-winged crossbills, a flock of muted reds and golds and greens, crawling all over the apex of a snowy spruce tree. They weighed less than an ounce apiece, they'd been outdoors all winter, they were flashy in their feather coats, the spruce cones were apparently delicious to them, and even as I envied them their sociability in the snow I worried for their safety in the for-profit future now plotted by the conservatives in Washington. In this future, a small percentage of people will win the big prize—the Lincoln Navigator, the mansion with a two-story atrium and a five-acre lawn, the second home in Laguna Beach—and everybody else will be offered electronic simulacra of luxuries to wish for. The obvious difficulty for crossbills in this future is that crossbills don't *want* the Navigator. They don't *want* the atrium or the amenities of Laguna. What crossbills want is boreal forests where they can crack open seed cones with their parrot-of-the-northland bills. When our atmospheric carbon raises global temperatures by another five degrees, and our remaining unlogged boreal forests succumb to insects emboldened by the shorter winters, and crossbills run out of places to live, the "ownership society" isn't going to help them. Their standard of living won't be improvable by global free trade. Not even the pathetic state lottery will be an option for them then.

In Florida, at the Estero Lagoon at Fort Myers Beach, where, according to my guidebook, I was likely to find "hundreds" of red knots and Wilson's plovers, I instead found a Jimmy Buffett song playing on the Holiday Inn beachfront sound system and a flock of gulls loitering on the white sand behind the hotel. It was happy hour. As I was scanning the flock, making sure that it consisted entirely of ring-billed gulls and laughing gulls, a tourist came over to take pictures. She kept moving closer, absorbed in her snapshots, and the flock amoebically distanced itself from her, some of the gulls hopping a little in their haste, the group murmuring uneasily and finally breaking into alarm cries as the woman bore down with her pocket digital camera. How, I wondered, could she not see that the gulls only wanted to be left alone? Then again, the gulls didn't seem to mind the Jimmy Buffett. The animal who most clearly wanted to be left alone was me. Farther down the beach, still looking for the promised throngs of red knots and Wilson's plovers, I came upon a particularly charmless stretch of muddy

sand on which there were a handful of more common shore-
birds, dunlins and semipalmated plovers and least sandpipers,
in their brownish-gray winter plumage. Camped out amid
high-rise condos and hotels, surveying the beach in postures of
sleepy disgruntlement, with their heads scrunched down and
their eyes half shut, they looked like a little band of misfits. Like
a premonition of a future in which all birds will either collabo-
rate with modernity or go off to die someplace quietly. What
I felt for them went beyond love. I felt outright identification.
The well-adjusted throngs of collaborator birds in South
Florida, both the trash pigeons and trash grackles and the more
stately but equally tame pelicans and cormorants, all struck me
now as traitors. It was this motley band of modest peeps and
plovers on the beach who reminded me of the human beings I
loved best—the ones who didn't fit in. These birds may or may
not have been capable of emotion, but the way they looked, be-
leaguered there, few in number, my outcast friends, was how I
felt. I'd been told that it was bad to anthropomorphize, but I
could no longer remember why. It was, in any case, anthropo-
morphic only to see yourself in other species, not to see them in
yourself. To be hungry all the time, to be mad for sex, to not believe in global warming, to be shortsighted, to live without
thought of your grandchildren, to spend half your life on personal grooming, to be perpetually on guard, to be compulsive,
to be habit-bound, to be avid, to be unimpressed with humanity, to prefer your own kind: these were all ways of being like a
bird. Later in the evening, in posh, necropolitan Naples, on a
sidewalk outside a hotel whose elevator doors were decorated
with huge blowups of cute children and the monosyllabic in-
junction SMILE, I spotted two disaffected teenagers, two little
chicks, in full Goth plumage, and I wished that I could introduce them to the brownish-gray misfits on the beach.

. . .

A few weeks after I heard Al Gore speak at the Ethical Culture Society, I went back to Texas. According to my new AviSys 5.0 bird-listing software, the green kingfisher that I'd seen in the last hour of my trip with Manley had been my 370th North American bird. I was close to the satisfying milestone of four hundred species, and the easiest way to reach it without waiting around for spring migration was to go south again.

I also missed Texas. For a person with a bird problem, there was something oddly reassuring about the place. The lower Rio Grande Valley contained some of the ugliest land I'd ever seen: dead flat expanses of industrial farming and downmarket sprawl bisected by U.S. Route 83, which was a jerry-rigged viaduct flanked by three-lane frontage roads, Whataburgers, warehouses, billboards suggesting VAGINAL REJUVENATION and FAITH PLEASES GOD and DON'T DUMP ("Take your trash to a landfill"), rotten town centers where only the Payless shoe stores seemed to be in business, and fake-adobe strip malls so pristinely bleak it was hard to tell if they were still being built or had already opened and gone bankrupt. And yet, to birds, the valley was a Michelin three-star destination: Worth a Journey! Texas was the home of President Bush and House Majority Leader Tom DeLay, neither of whom had ever been mistaken for a friend of the environment; its property owners were famously hostile to federal regulation; and yet it was the state where, with some serious driving, you could tally 230 species of bird in a single day. There were thriving Audubon Societies, the world's biggest birding-tour operator, special campgrounds and RV parks for birders, twenty annual birding festivals, and the Great Texas Coastal Birding Trail, which snaked for twenty-one hundred miles around petrochemical installations and supertanker hulls and giant citrus farms, from Port Charles to

Laredo. Texans didn't seem to lose much sleep over the division between nature and civilization. Even ardent bird lovers in Texas referred to birds collectively as "the resource." Texans liked to use the oxymoron "wildlife management." They were comfortable with hunting and viewed birding as basically a nonviolent version of it. They gave me blank, dumbfounded looks when I asked them if they identified with birds and felt a kinship with them, or whether, on the contrary, they saw birds as beings very different from themselves. They asked me to repeat the question.

I flew into McAllen. After revisiting the refuges I'd hit with Manley and bagging specialties like the pauraque (No. 374), the elf owl (No. 379), and the fulvous whistling-duck (No. 383), I drove north to a scrap of state land where the black-capped vireo (No. 388) and golden-cheeked warbler (No. 390), two endangered species, were helpfully singing out their locations. Much of my best birding, however, took place on private land. A friend of a friend's friend gave me a tour of his eight-thousand-acre ranch near Waco, letting me pick up three new inland sandpiper species on wetlands that the federal government had paid him to create. On the King Ranch, whose land holdings are larger than Rhode Island and include a hundred thousand acres of critical coastal habitat for migrating songbirds, I paid $119 for the opportunity to see my first ferruginous pygmy-owl and my first northern beardless-tyrannulet. North of Harlingen, I visited other friends of friends' friends, a pediatric dentist and his wife who had created a private wildlife refuge for themselves on five thousand acres of mesquite. The couple had dug a lake, converted old hunting blinds to nature-photography blinds, and planted big flower beds to attract birds and butterflies. They told me about their efforts to reeducate certain of their landowning neighbors who, like my father in the seventies, had been alienated by environmental bureaucrats.

To be Texan was to take pride in the beauty and diversity of Texan wildlife, and the couple believed that the conservationist spirit in most Texan ranchers just needed a little coaxing out.

This, of course, was an axiom of movement conservatism—if you get government off people's back, they'll gladly take responsibility—and it seemed to me both wishful and potentially self-serving. At a distance, in New York, through the fog of contemporary politics, I probably would have identified the dentist and his wife, who were Bush supporters, as my enemies. But the picture was trickier in close-up. For one thing, I was liking all the Texans I met. I was also beginning to wonder whether, poor though birds are, they might prefer to take their chances in a radically privatized America where income distribution is ever more unequal, the estate tax is repealed, and land-proud Texan ranchers are able to preserve their oak mottes and vast mesquite thickets and lease them out to wealthy hunters. It certainly was pleasant to bird on a private ranch! Far away from the picnickers and the busloads of schoolkids! Far from the bikers, the off-roaders, the dog walkers, the smoochers, the dumpers, the partyers, the bird-indifferent masses! The fences that kept them out were no impediment to thrushes and wrens.

It was on federal property, though, that I got my four-hundredth species. In the village of Rockport, on Aransas Bay, I boarded a shallow-draft birding boat, the *Skimmer*, which was captained by an affable young outdoorsman named Tommy Moore. My fellow passengers were some eager older women and their silent husbands. If they'd been picnicking in a place where I had a rarity staked out, I might not have liked them, but they were on the *Skimmer* to look at birds. As we cut across the bay's shallow, cement-gray waters and bore down on the roosting site of a dozen great blue herons—birds so common I hardly noticed them anymore—the women began to wail with astonishment and pleasure: "Oh! Oh! What magnificent birds! Oh! Look at them! Oh my God!"

We pulled up alongside a very considerable green salt marsh. In the distance, hip-deep in salt grass, were two adult whooping cranes whose white breasts and long, sturdy necks and russet heads reflected sunlight that then passed through my binoculars and fell upon my retinas, allowing me to claim the crane as my No. 400. One of the animals was bending down as if concerned about something in the tall grass; the other seemed to be scanning the horizon anxiously. Their attitude reminded me of parent birds I'd seen in distress elsewhere—two bluejays in the Ramble fluttering in futile, crazed rage while a raccoon ate their eggs; a jittery, too-alert loon sitting shoulder-deep in water by the side of a badly flooded Minnesota lake, persisting in incubating eggs that weren't going to hatch—and Captain Moore explained that harm appeared to have befallen the year-ling child of these two cranes; they'd been standing in the same place for more than a day, the young crane nowhere to be seen.

"Could it be dead?" one of the women asked.

"The parents wouldn't still be there if it had died," Moore said. He took out his radio and called in a report on the birds to the Aransas National Wildlife Refuge office, which told him that the chief crane biologist was on his way out to investigate.

"In fact," Moore told us, stowing the radio, "there he is."

Half a mile away, on the far side of a shallow salt pool, keeping his head low and moving very slowly, was a speck of a human figure. The sight of him there, in stringently protected federal territory, was disconcerting in the way of a boom mike dipping into a climactic movie scene, a stagehand wandering around behind Jason and Medea. Must humankind insert itself into *everything*? Having paid thirty-five dollars for my ticket, I'd expected a more perfect illusion of nature.

The biologist himself, inching toward the cranes, alone in his waders, didn't look as if he felt any embarrassment. It was simply his job to try to keep the whooping crane from going extinct. And this job, in one sense, was fairly hopeless. There were currently fewer than 350 wild whooping cranes on the planet, and although the figure was definitely an improvement on the 1941 population of 22, the long-term outlook for any species with such a small gene pool was dismal. The entire Aransas reserve was one melted Greenland ice cap away from being suitable for waterskiing, one severe storm away from being a killing field. Nevertheless, as Captain Moore cheerfully informed us, scientists had been taking eggs from the cranes' nests in western Canada and incubating them in Florida, where there was now a wholly manufactured second flock of more than thirty birds, and since whooping cranes don't naturally know the way to migrate (each new generation learns the route by following its parents), scientists had been trying to teach the cranes in Florida to follow an airplane to a second summering site in Wisconsin . . .

To know that something is doomed and to cheerfully try to save it anyway: it was a characteristic of my mother. I had finally started to love her near the end of her life, when she was undergoing a year of chemotherapy and radiation and living by herself. I'd admired her bravery for that. I'd admired her will to recuperate and her extraordinary tolerance of pain. I'd felt proud when her sister remarked to me, "Your mother looks better two days after abdominal surgery than I do at a dinner party." I'd admired her skill and ruthlessness at the bridge table, where she wore the same determined frown when she had everything under control as when she knew she was going down. The last decade of her life, which started with my father's dementia and ended with her colon cancer, was a rotten hand that she played like a winner. Even toward the end, though, I couldn't tolerate being with her for more than three days at a time. Although she was my last living link to a web of Midwestern relations and traditions that I would begin to miss the moment she was gone, and although the last time I saw her in her house, in April 1999, her cancer was back and she was rapidly losing weight, I still took care to arrive in St. Louis on a Friday afternoon and leave on a Monday night. She, for her part, was accustomed to my leavings and didn't complain too much. But she still felt about me what she'd always felt, which was what I wouldn't really feel about her until after she was gone. "I hate it when Daylight Savings Time starts while you're here," she told me while we were driving to the airport, "because it means I have an hour less with you."

As the *Skimmer* moved up the channel, we were able to approach other cranes close enough to hear them crunching on blue crabs, the staple of their winter diet. We saw a pair doing the prancing, graceful, semiairborne dance that gets them sexually excited. Following the lead of my fellow passengers, I took out my camera and dutifully snapped some pictures. But all of a sudden—it might have been my having reached the empty plateau of four hundred species—I felt weary of birds and birding. For the moment at least, I was ready to be home in New York again, home among my kind. Every happy day with the Californian made the dimensions of our future losses a little more grievous, every good hour sharpened my sadness at how fast our lives were going, how rapidly death was coming out to meet us, but I still couldn't wait to see her: to set down my bags inside the door, to go and find her in her study, where she would probably be chipping away at her interminable e-mail queue, and to hear her say, as she always said when I came home, "So? What did you see?"